What Dare I Think

Julian Huxley

Nabu Public Domain Reprints:

You are holding a reproduction of an original work published before 1923 that is in the public domain in the United States of America, and possibly other countries. You may freely copy and distribute this work as no entity (individual or corporate) has a copyright on the body of the work. This book may contain prior copyright references, and library stamps (as most of these works were scanned from library copies). These have been scanned and retained as part of the historical artifact.

This book may have occasional imperfections such as missing or blurred pages, poor pictures, errant marks, etc. that were either part of the original artifact, or were introduced by the scanning process. We believe this work is culturally important, and despite the imperfections, have elected to bring it back into print as part of our continuing commitment to the preservation of printed works worldwide. We appreciate your understanding of the imperfections in the preservation process, and hope you enjoy this valuable book.

OSMANIA UNIVERSITY LIBRARY

Call No. Accession No.

Author Huxley, Julian 1818

Title What dare I think.

This book should be returned on or before the date last marked below.

WHAT DARE I THINK?
The Challenge of Modern Science
to Human Action and Belief

By

JULIAN HUXLEY

PROFESSOR OF ZOOLOGY
IN THE UNIVERSITY OF LONDON
(KING'S COLLEGE)

CHATTO AND WINDUS
LONDON

First published October 1931
Third edition January 1932
First issued in the Phoenix Library
1933

Printed in Great Britain : all rights reserved

PREFACE

I HAD first of all thought of calling this little work ' Essays in Scientific Humanism.' But the word *Essays* has not a very fashionable sound to-day, while the word *Humanism* has of late years been a good deal overdone, especially in the United States, where further it has acquired a slightly different connotation from that which it bears in England. And, finally, I discovered that another book had recently been published with the phrase *Scientific Humanism* in its title.

So there was nothing to do but to try and think of a new name. But whatever the actual title, what this book really contains is some *Essays in Scientific Humanism*. By saying that they are Essays I mean that they were not all written on the same occasion ; but by saying that they are essays in a particular subject I mean that, in spite of this discontinuity of composition, they are definitely tied together by a common attitude of mind, a common approach. Finally, by using the phrase Scientific Humanism, I mean something perfectly definite, which I hope will emerge clearly from Chapters IV. and V. I am sorry that the word *humanism* has been distorted in the United States, on the one hand to mean a philosophical doctrine which does not seem to me particularly humanistic in any recognized sense, and on the other to serve as the name for an interesting brand of anti-supernatural religion. For in its undistorted natural sense it is very useful; and I see no other phrase but *Scientific Humanism* which could conveniently be used to crystallize that attitude of mind which it seems to me so imperative for the modern world to cultivate.

The first five chapters are an amplification of three lectures which I was invited to give before the Henry LaBarre Jayne Foundation in Philadelphia in January 1931. The plan of them remains unaltered, but they have been considerably revised and amplified for purposes of publication. Chapters IV. and V. can also be regarded as an amplification

PREFACE

of a lecture on Scientific Humanism delivered in 1930 as President of the Social and Political Education League. The final chapters were written as the Conway Memorial Lecture which the Ethical Society invited me to give in October 1930. The Conway Lecture was, as is customary, reprinted in booklet form and published by the Rationalist Press Association. Portions of some of the other lectures have appeared in the *Contemporary Review*, the *Atlantic Monthly*, and the *Yale Review*. To the editors and publishers concerned, I would like to tender my thanks for permission to reprint these articles.

In conclusion, I would like to thank the Ethical Society, the Social and Political Education League, and especially the Trustees of the Henry LaBarre Jayne Foundation for their invitations to lecture under their auspices; without these I should not have had the stimulus to bring my scattered ideas into some sort of order, and this book would never have been written.

King's College,
    London, *June* 1931.

TABLE OF CONTENTS

I Biology and the Physical Environment of Man   *Page* 1

II Biology and the Human Individual   45

III Man and His Heredity   74

IV The Conflict between Science and Human Nature   121

V Scientific Humanism   149

VI Science, Religion and Human Nature   178

VII Science and the Future of Religion   224

CHAPTER I

Biology and the Physical Environment of Man

SCIENCES, like Empires, have their rise and their time of flourishing, though not their decay. Naturally, the order of their rise runs parallel with the complexity of their subject-matter. The physical sciences, being the simplest and most straightforward, were the first to start their triumphant career. Some time in the future it will be the turn of psychology and of the elusive social sciences; but at the moment the chief upward movement is that of biology.

Looked at with the eye of the historian of science, biology is seen to be just reaching the position attained by the physico-chemical sciences about the middle of last century. The phase in which that branch of science then found itself was one in which a number of different lines of investigation were being brought into intimate and often unexpected relations, in which several separate sets of concepts were being federated into a single, embracing scheme. Heat had come to be envisaged, in Tyndall's phrase, as a 'mode of motion'; the kinetic theory of gases tied the atoms of the chemist and the physicist's laws of temperature and pressure into a single whole. The generalizing of electro-magnetic theory; the cohesion given to apparently unrelated subjects by the principle of the Conservation of Energy; the unity afforded to chemical facts by Mendeléeff's Periodic Law—these were some of the ideas which were unifying physico-chemical science.

Similarly to-day in biology, the distribution of hereditary qualities is seen to be a special aspect of cytology, of the behaviour of the contents of the cell as seen with the new eye provided by the microscope. Mind and body are revealed with ever-increasing clearness as two sides of the single biological reality, the organism, and not to be disentangled from each other. The ductless glands which control the chemistry of our bodies influence also the activity of our souls, adjust the development of our embryo selves, and are one of the important means by which the hereditary constitution impresses itself upon our natures. Evolution is becoming more intelligible as we link up the facts derived from the breeding-pen, the fossils in the rocks, the behaviour of developing embryos and larvæ, the laws of growth, the scientific study of natural history, the manœuvres of the chromosomes, and the distribution of animals and plants over the world's surface, not forgetting to call in the discipline of mathematics to our aid. Medicine and physiology are unified by ideas drawn from evolution and experimental embryology. In brief, it is no longer possible to be a physiologist or a biochemist, an ecologist or a morphologist, a geneticist or a systematist (or at least not possible to do good work in any of these sub-sciences) without knowing a good deal of other branches of biology as well.

Looked at from the standpoint of applied science (and science always has its two aspects, its intellectual aspect as knowledge and its practical aspect as control), the present position of biology appears equally distinctive. Every science arrives at a stage during which it makes its main broad contributions to practical human affairs. Biology is clearly on the verge of such a phase, while it is already over for physics and chemistry, and psychology and sociology cannot hope to reach it for perhaps another century.

I do not in the least mean to imply that practical inventions and applications of the utmost benefit and importance will not continue to be made in the purely physico-chemical sphere for millennia to come. Of course they will. But the chief kinds of things which man has wanted to ask of this kind of science have already been granted. Man has wished to travel fast: he is already approaching the mechanical and physiological limits of speed. He has wished to communicate with other men at a distance, to capture and store the treasures of sight and hearing; and there are the telegraph and the telephone, the radio and the gramophone,

BIOLOGY AND PHYSICAL ENVIRONMENT

the photograph and the motion picture. He has wanted to fly in the air like a bird and swim under the water like a fish : he can and does. He has wished to be able to synthetize useful substances, to apply power with an intensity or speed a thousand-fold or million-fold of that possible to his own unaided forces, to turn night into day at will, to make machines do his mechanical work for him : he has already in large and indeed undreamt-of measure succeeded.

But when we come to the biological field, the picture is very different. Most of us would like to live longer; to have healthier and happier lives; to be able to control the sex of our children when they are conceived, and afterwards to mould their bodies, intellects and temperaments into the best possible forms; to reduce unnecessary pain to a minimum ; to be able at will to whip up our energies to their fullest pitch without later ill effects. It would be pleasant to be able to manufacture new kinds of animals and plants at our pleasure, like so many chemical compounds, to double the yield of an acre of wheat or a herd of cattle, to keep the balance of nature adjusted in our favour, to banish parasites and disease germs from the world. And there have been Utopians from Plato's time and before it, most of whom have dreamt of controlling the stream of the race itself—not merely in its volume and quantity, but in its quality, so that humanity would blossom into a new character.

Of these obvious biological aspirations, how many have been fulfilled? Anaesthetics remove some of the grosser tortures of pain; the average span of life is a few years longer; some diseases have been stamped out or rendered less dangerous enemies; there has been some progress in the moulding of our animals and crops and flowers. But in general the wishes have remained only wishes.

On the other hand, enough knowledge is there to make it clear that these biological wishes will soon be ripe for fulfilment. And their fulfilment will obviously have more intimate and more radical effects than the fulfilment of chemical and mechanical wishes,

BIOLOGY AND PHYSICAL ENVIRONMENT

for it will be affecting men directly instead of indirectly.

I do not share the facile optimism which sees in every increase of power, every fulfilment of a wish, a necessary good. The knowledge provided by science is emotionally and morally neutral. And so is the power of control which inevitably arises out of that knowledge. It is a tool, which like other tools can be used for whatever ends its possessor sees fit, whether good, bad or indifferent. The effects of the industrial revolution and the subsequent inventions in the physico-chemical sphere have not been so rosy as to warrant the belief—still, it would appear, widely held—that every invention is inevitably good, and that progress is automatic. Progress is only automatic in the sense that man, once he has reached a certain stage in his development, cannot be kept from exerting his faculties and making new discoveries ; but it is not automatic in the sense of being a process inflicted upon us inevitably from without, independent of our efforts and ideals. Thus, while it is futile to try and turn back the tide, it is shallow folly to sit back complacently and watch its course. The true optimism is a tempered one. Change must come; it can, on balance, be good; it is our business to try to guide it and ensure that it shall be not merely change but progress.

An excellent example to our purpose is afforded by the biological sources of power. With the gradual exhaustion of coal and oil, better chemical methods, and the improvement of tropical agriculture, more and more of the combustible sources of power, such as the alcohols, will be got from the tropics, manufactured out of plants. This will mean a revolution, a major shift in the economic system of the world. The last great economic revolution was the industrial revolution; and one of its effects was the growth of an industrial proletariat, which has not been without its disastrous results, disastrous politically and perhaps more, in the long run, socially and racially. If we are content in this forthcoming economic revolution once again to adopt a *laissez-faire* attitude, the world will

BIOLOGY AND PHYSICAL ENVIRONMENT

have on its hands a new proletariat, agricultural instead of industrial, tropical instead of temperate, black and brown instead of white; and the results of its growth will be equally disastrous.

That is a good example, because it illustrates how the various aspects of a problem can never be separated from each other. Power from tropical vegetation will never be a commercial proposition until economic pressure joins hands with chemical skill, with the biologist's tricks for controlling weeds and insect pests, the plant-breeder's manufacture of new types of organism, the agriculturist's control of the soil; and once it enters the commercial field, it will immediately affect the structure of the world's economic framework, the social life and, in the long run, the biological characteristics of the primitive peoples of the tropics, and the whole race and colour problem.

In the brief space at my disposal I have not the room, even if I had the knowledge, to explore these far-reaching inter-relations of biological progress with all other human activities. I must content myself with reminding my readers that they are always there, urging them to let their social and human imagination play round the consequences of scientific fact.

Let us take a couple of examples at random to point the moral, and then continue with the plain tale of biology. It is clearly desirable for man to be more healthy; and with regard to all the numerous brood of germ-caused diseases, the most obvious way of attempting to provide more health is by getting rid of the germ. I say the most obvious way; it may not prove to be the most practicable way. The League of Nations Commission on Malaria in Europe laid down as its first principle that the radical elimination of the malaria-transmitting mosquito was not practical politics; and there can be no reasonable being who can imagine it possible to get rid of tuberculosis germs out of the world within the next thousand years. But, in some cases, we could eliminate the germ, either locally, in the more civilized countries, or in some cases, even universally.

BIOLOGY AND PHYSICAL ENVIRONMENT

Yellow fever is fighting a losing battle with Mr Rockefeller; it should, in the long run, be possible to wipe out the trypanosomes of sleeping sickness; scarlet fever and diphtheria, typhoid and enteric can be killed out or reduced to negligible proportions in really civilized countries.

Well and good: but are all the results necessarily good? In the first place, with the lifting of the rigorous hand of selection, the natural immunity to these diseases would decrease with their decrease. Before measles were known in the South Seas, there was no biological necessity for the South Sea Islanders to possess any immunity to the disease, and there were among them all grades of inborn and inheritable resistance, from zero to moderately high. When it was introduced, it killed like the Black Death; and by the elimination of those with least natural resistance, the average resistance of the race has been considerably raised. And the converse will hold: with the banishing of a disease, the biological need for resistance will disappear, the less resistant will survive just as well as the more resistant, and the average resistance of the population will gradually go down.

What will then happen if the disease is reintroduced after several centuries of banishment? It might be reintroduced during a war by an unscrupulous enemy; it might get in accidentally; the nation might decline and pay less attention to sanitation, so that the barriers to the entry of the disease-germs were lowered. And in any such event, the disease would race through the country like flame through dry grass, killing by the tens of thousands.

What we have been saying applies to specific resistance-immunity to one particular disease-germ, not necessarily correlated with immunity to any other disease, nor with general vigour. But there is also general, non-specific resistance, something to do with general health and vigour, the broad scale against which the narrow scales of specific resistances are set up. *Ceteris paribus*, the strong and generally healthy child or man will survive, the weakling will succumb. And

BIOLOGY AND PHYSICAL ENVIRONMENT

if many diseases were banished from a country, and matters otherwise left to themselves, it is almost certain that there would be a lowering of the general vitality, stamina, and resistance of the population through the disproportionate survival of the weaker vessels whom the diseases would have eliminated more ruthlessly than they did the general population; the population would be healthier as regards these particular diseases, but as a race it would have put its foot on the downward slope of degeneration.

Or take another example, more spectacular, if more remote. The discovery that sex is determined at conception by means of the existence of two kinds of male cells, male-determining and female-determining, of which the female-determiners are a little the bigger owing to their possession of an extra chromosome, opens the door to a possible control of sex. This could only be done through a separation of the two kinds of male cells, and the subsequent injection of one or the other; thus it is not likely to become widespread, even if it should become practicable, in our type of society. But five hundred years hence such interferences with nature may be regarded in the same matter-of-fact way as we regard interferences with nature which we now practise, like drinking the milk of other species of animal, using telephones and aeroplanes, or wearing clothes. And then the sociological implications will begin. Should it be in the power of any parent to regulate the sex of his offspring at will? If so, would not there be a great over-production of males? If, on the other hand, it were left to the State, would there not again be a great over-production of males, for purely militaristic reasons? And, in such case, would this not lead to what we might call a bootlegging production of girl children, privately and illicitly? For we can be sure that if there is a shortage of any essential commodity, human or otherwise, the production of that commodity will become immensely profitable.

So we might go on; but I have said enough to show how important it is not to work in watertight compartments, but to try to anticipate the consequences of any change, the reverberations of science upon economics, recreation or social life.

So much by way of introduction. In what follows, the scheme I have adopted to bring some order into my facts is itself a biological one. I have tried to describe some of the influences which biology is exerting or might exert, first upon the tangible environment in which man lives; next upon men and women as individuals; then upon man as a continuing race; and last upon that intangible environment which man alone of all organisms possesses, the tradition of thought and customs and accumulated ideas to which, just as inevitably and rigorously as to the physical environment, his growing nature must adapt itself.

The most obvious way in which biological science can have its practical say is in its effect upon the environment of man. Not only can it influence this or that particular kind of animal or plant, encouraging one, destroying another, re-modelling a third, but it must be called in to adjust the balance of nature.

WHAT DARE I THINK?

The balance of nature is a very elaborate and very delicate system of checks and counterchecks. It is continually being altered as climates change, as new organisms evolve, as animals or plants permeate to new areas. But the alterations have in the past, for the most part, been slow, whereas with the arrival of man, and especially of civilized man, their speed has been multiplied many fold: from the evolutionary time-scale, where change is measured by periods of ten or a hundred thousand years, they have been transferred to the human time-scale in which centuries and even decades count.

Everywhere man is altering the balance of nature. He is facilitating the spread of plants and animals into new regions, sometimes deliberately, sometimes unconsciously. He is covering huge areas with new kinds of plants, or with houses, factories, slag-heaps and other products of his civilization. He exterminates some species on a large scale, but favours the multiplication of others. In brief, he has done more in five thousand years to alter the biological aspect

BIOLOGY AND PHYSICAL ENVIRONMENT

of the planet than has nature in five million.

Many of these changes which he has brought about have had unforeseen consequences. Who would have thought that the throwing away of a piece of Canadian waterweed would have caused half the waterways of Britain to be blocked for a decade? or that the provision of pot cacti for lonely settlers' wives would have led to Eastern Australia being overrun with forests of Prickly Pear? Who would have prophesied that the cutting down of forests on the Adriatic coasts, or in parts of Central Africa, could have reduced the land to a semi-desert, with the very soil washed away from the bare rock? Who would have thought that improved communications would have changed history by the spreading of disease—sleeping sickness into East Africa, measles into Oceania, very possibly malaria into ancient Greece?

These are spectacular examples; but examples on a smaller scale are everywhere to be found. We make a nature sanctuary for rare birds, prescribing absolute security for all species; and we may find that some common and hardy kind of bird multiplies beyond measure and ousts the rare kinds in which we were particularly interested. We see, owing to some little change brought about by civilization, the starling spread over the English countryside in hordes. We improve the yielding capacities of our cattle; and find that now they exhaust the pastures which sufficed for less exigent stock. We gaily set about killing the carnivores that molest our domestic animals, the hawks that eat our fowls and game-birds; and find that in so doing we are also removing the brake that restrains the multiplication of mice and other little rodents that gnaw away the farmers' profits.

In brief, our human activities are everywhere altering nature and its balance, whether we realize it or no, and whether we want to or no. If we do not wish the alterations to be chaotic, disorderly and often harmful, we must do our best to control them, and constitute new balances to suit our purposes.

BIOLOGY AND PHYSICAL ENVIRONMENT

The first and most obvious department of control is the conservation of nature and its resources. It is extremely easy to kill the goose that lays the golden eggs; and when the goose is a wild species, once killed it is gone for ever. The Maoris killed the Moas, of which a number of different kinds used to inhabit New Zealand, for their meat. Sailors exterminated the Great Auk. The final extinction of the Mammoths was in all probability caused by the attacks of our Stone Age ancestors. The white man reduced the Bison from an abundance comparable with the abundance of zebra or gnu in Africa until to-day its precarious remnant has to be looked after like a museum specimen. The Fur Seals of the Pacific were brought by indiscriminate slaughter to the verge of disappearance, and were only saved by international agreement. The huge hordes of whales of the northern seas were harried into insignificance; and now there is danger that their southern relatives will follow suit. Of the elephants of Africa, according to Major Hingston, ten per cent. are killed every year. The marvellous guano deposits of the west coast of South America were being exhausted, and have only been saved by the careful regulations at last imposed by the Peruvian Government.

If we want wild creatures to go on providing us with oil, furs, fertilizers, ivory, meat or sport, we must regulate their affairs as we would regulate a business. We must know where and when they breed, how many young they have, how long they take to grow up, what their natural mortality is, and must on the basis of this knowledge adjust our exploitation so that it only skims off the natural increase. This has been done for some animals; it can be done for those others that are now in danger of our reckless methods.

But as well as the preservation of particular species, there is the preservation of nature as a whole to think about. If we do not take care, we shall find civilization infiltrating all but the most inhospitable parts of our planet and leaving no regions in their pristine and exhilarating state. It is so easy to kill out game, leaving a country still untamed but sadly barren; to dot the wilderness with straggling outliers of industrialism, leaving it neither wild nor yet civilized; to cut down forests without making provision for replacement, leaving scrub forests of second growth, as over so much of the United States, or even only bare hillsides; in brief, to mix nature and civilization so that the fine essence of the one is destroyed, of the other not fully realized, and the net result an unsatisfying compromise.

The remedy is conscious planning. No one supposes that the game animals of Africa can everywhere remain as they are, that forests and jungles will not often need to be cut down, or replanted artificially and scientifically, that many swamps should not be drained, many stretches of sea-coast turned into holiday towns. But we can delimit different areas for different purposes. Man does not live by bread alone. There is his need for solitude to consider, and his scientific interests; there is the recreation and refreshment afforded to him by nature, and the unique excitement and interest of seeing wild creatures.

WHAT DARE I THINK?

These needs can all be met if we only take them in time. There are different balances of nature and civilization, each of them admirable in its way, whose preservation can be deliberately planned. We can plan the city so that it provides beauty, ease of movement, varied activities, and a sense of civic pride. We can plan the small town so that it provides a centre of life for its area, yet without spoiling the zone of country round it. The real countryside is profoundly artificial, with nature tamed by man; but it represents a particular balance, which has its own unique possibilities of beauty and interest, and it can be guarded from unwarranted intrusions, its peculiar attractions can be preserved, its development can be guided. The half-wild country of moor, mountain, marsh, forest or sea-shore can be either entirely reclaimed, or kept entirely unspoilt.

When we come to setting aside definite tracts of land for other than material needs, we can plan them with precise aims in view. Some areas should be set apart as specimens of nature, just as we preserve specimens of interesting animals and plants in our museums. These are Nature Sanctuaries, to which access should only be sparingly accorded, and then mainly for purposes of scientific study. The prime object here is to keep the original balance as unaltered as possible. Then there are National Parks, where nature is conserved not in the interests of the enquiring scientific spirit of man, but in the interests of his love of natural beauty and need of wildness and solitude. The essentials of nature must here be preserved, but a compromise will often have to be struck with the need for making nature accessible. All grades of naturalness can be preserved in National Parks, from the unspoilt wildness of the Grisons or the Yosemite to the partially-tamed beauties of Sussex downland or the New Forest. And, finally, we can provide scheduled areas; for these, while recognizing that their prime purpose is utilitarian, we can introduce regulations which will ensure that their wild life and their other attractions are interfered with as little as may be, and that their possibilities of providing recreation and beauty are made plentifully available.

In addition to these main categories, we may establish reserves for special purposes—for bird life, for the preservation of rare or beautiful plants, or even for strange human beings like the pigmies. But in every case we must have in mind just what we want to do, and carry out our plans accordingly. In almost every case some degree of control will be needed to preserve this or that balance, for the original balance of nature is gone, destroyed by the mere presence of man on earth; and even in the remotest regions it will rarely be enough to leave everything to nature, for nature almost everywhere has already been in some measure modified by man, and is therefore already to that extent artificial. I will give but one illustration. The traveller through East Africa naturally thinks that its great stretches of thorn-scrub country are a part of primeval nature. But in great part they exist by virtue of human interference; if it were not for the black man's cattle, and his habit of burning the

BIOLOGY AND PHYSICAL ENVIRONMENT

bush, they would be woodland, of quite a different character. Those who want other examples will find them in abundance in Ritchie's interesting book, *The Influence of Man on Animal Life in Scotland*. Even to preserve nature, we need to have a knowledge of the machinery by which the balance of nature is adjusted; and for that we need a well-developed science of ecology, that branch of biology which studies the relations of wild organisms to each other and to their environment.

The other province of ecological biology is its aid, not in preserving nature as near her original self as possible, but in controlling and remoulding her to suit the economic purposes of man.

Agriculture is the chief of man's efforts at the biological remodelling of nature. If we reflect that agriculture is less than a paltry ten thousand years old out of the three hundred million years that green plants have been on earth, and that apart from forest fires and perhaps a little occasional clearing, there had before that been no human interference with the natural mantle of vegetation, we begin to grasp something of the revolution wrought by this biological discovery.

But agriculture is, if you like, unnatural; it concentrates innumerable individuals of a single species—and always, of course, a particularly nutritious one—in serried ranks, while nature's method is to divide up the space among numerous competing or complementary kinds. Thus it constitutes not merely an opportunity but a veritable invitation to vegetable-feeding animals, of which the most numerous and most difficult to control are the small, insinuating and rapidly-multiplying insects. And the better and more intensive the agriculture, the richer becomes the banquet, the more obvious the invitation. Shifting cultivation, with poorly-developed crop-plants and plenty of weeds, is one thing; but mile upon square mile of tender, well-weeded wheat or tea or cotton offers the optimum possibilities for the rapid multiplication and spread of any species of insect which can take advantage of man's good nature towards his kind.

BIOLOGY AND PHYSICAL ENVIRONMENT

Finally, man's insatiable desire for rapid and easy transit has capped the trouble. Evil communications, we all know, corrupt good manners: it is not generally realized how much good communications have done to corrupt the balance of nature.

By accident or intention, animal and plant species find their way along the trade routes to new countries. They are in a new environment, among a new set of competing creatures to whose particular equilibrium of struggle they are not adapted. In such circumstances, the majority fail to gain a foothold at all; some survive on sufferance; but a few find in the new circumstances a release instead of a hindrance, and multiply beyond measure. The release may be a release from competitors, as when the mongoose was introduced into one of the West Indian islands, or, more frequently, a release from enemies, whether large and predatory or small and parasitic.

Then it is up to the biologist to see what his knowledge can do. Can he, by studying the pest in its original home, discover what are the other species that normally act as checks on its over-multiplication, make sure that, if he imports them to the new country, they will not there change their habits and turn into pests themselves, then successfully transport them, and breed them and let them loose in sufficient numbers to bring the enemy of the crops down to insignificance? Sometimes he can. Let me give two examples. On Fiji, coconuts have for some time been one of the staple products. Some few decades ago, the plantations on one of the main islands were reduced to nutless, leafless poles. That was bad enough; but then, after the war, the plague began to appear on the other and larger main island.

The men are still alive and active who brought prosperity back to Fiji. It had already been discovered that the cause of the trouble was a little moth—very beautiful, with violet wings—whose grubs devoured the leaves of the palm-trees; and it prospered so alarmingly because in Fiji it had no parasite enemies. Three biologists were appointed to find a parasite. They searched the remote

BIOLOGY AND PHYSICAL ENVIRONMENT

corners of the Pacific. At last they found, in the Malay States, not the same moth, but a closely-related species, which was provided with its natural complement of parasites, notably a kind of fly. It was not easy to bring the parasites the long distance to Fiji, for they do not hibernate, and so must be fed and tended all the time. They had to be provided with living moth-caterpillars, and these in return had to be provided with newly-sprouted coconuts, grown in specially-built cages. As there was no direct communication from this part of the Malay States to Fiji, a steamer had to be chartered for the voyage.

By these means, 300 precious parasitic flies were in 1925 safely landed in Fiji. These were bred on the caterpillars of the Fiji coconut moth, and within twelve months had increased to 32,000. Then the liberation of the parasites began, and they went to their work with such gusto that by 1928 at least four-fifths of the coconut-moth caterpillars of Fiji were parasitized, and therefore came to nothing. By 1929 the coconut moth, which threatened to ruin the archipelago, had become reduced to the status of a minor nuisance. Man had readjusted the environment, whose balance he had in the first instance upset.

Then there is the Prickly Pear in Eastern Australia. I remember once hearing a lecture by Dr Tillyard, now in charge of pest control and related problems in Australia. After he had been talking of the Prickly Pear for a bit, he drew out his watch. ' It is seven minutes,' he said, ' since I began discussing this subject ; during that time another seven acres of Australian land have been covered with this impenetrable and useless scrub.' That, however, was five or six years ago. In the meanwhile, the research scheme begun by the Australian Commonwealth in 1920 has matured. At their research station established on the American continent—original home of the prickly pear and other cacti— every possible enemy of the cactus was tried out ; and at last a mixed team was sent to Australia—a caterpillar to tunnel through the ' leaves ' (which are really the prickly

BIOLOGY AND PHYSICAL ENVIRONMENT

pear's stems), a plant bug and a cochineal insect to suck its juices, and a mite to scarify its surface. These were the Four Arthropods of the prickly pear's Apocalypse; instead of increasing any longer in Australia, it is now halted, and in many places the thickets are melting away under the combined attack.

One could multiply instances. How the sugar-cane of Hawaii was saved from its weevil destroyers; how the destruction of North American forests by Gipsy-moths was held in check; how an attack is being launched upon the mealy-bugs that are such a pest to Kenya coffee, by massed battalions of lady-birds, bred up on a generous ration consisting of chopped eggs, cream, marmite, honey, and radio-malt. To cope with all the demands for anti-pest organisms, a veritable industry has sprung up. There exists near Slough a Government establishment, usually nicknamed the Parasite Zoo, whose prime function is to breed up the supply of pest-parasites demanded by the British Empire.

All the spectacular successes have been achieved when a pest has invaded new territory ahead of its enemies. Even in such cases, however, success has not always been attained. Sometimes this may be due to the weakness of human nature: there have been Boards of Pest Control which were not too anxious to find their occupation gone with the going of their particular pest. But leaving such non-biological or hyper-biological considerations on one side, there have been many pests which have so far baffled research. One need only think of the invading thickets of blackberries in New Zealand; of the disease that has recently been blighting the elms in its march across Western Europe; of the spread of the European corn-borer over the United States to the great detriment of the maize crop; of the permanent pest of rabbits in Australia.

Such being the difficulties of the work when reduced to its simplest terms, we should expect to find them far more severe when the pest is an old-established inhabitant of the country. For then it will already possess its full complement of enemies and parasites, and exist in a natural equilibrium with them,

BIOLOGY AND PHYSICAL ENVIRONMENT

so that we can have little hope of causing a speedy reduction by the mere liberation of a parasite. And it has become a pest through man providing, in his own person or in that of his domestic animals or plants, a new and susceptible source of food. Problems of this type are set to us by malaria, spread by indigenous mosquitoes; human sleeping sickness and nagana disease of cattle, transmitted by tsetse-flies; plague, dependent for its spread upon the ubiquitous rat.

In British Africa alone, areas aggregating many times the size of Great Britain are infested by tsetse, and so made uninhabitable by any native population save hunting nomads, since all settled native culture involves the keeping of cattle. In some places, the issue is whether man or the fly shall dominate the country; at the present moment the fly's dominion in Tanganyika is twice the size of man's. The disease-agents which it transmits, the blood-parasites called trypanosomes, live normally in the blood of game and other wild animals, and do them no harm, since host and parasite have become mutually adapted through millennia of selective adjustment ; but man and his beasts are new hosts, and are without any such adaptive resistance. In such a case, the best remedy seems to be to alter the whole environment in such a way that the tsetse can no longer happily live in it. Most tsetse-flies live in bush country. They cannot exist either in quite open country, or in cultivated land, or in dense woodland or forest. So that either wholesale clearing or afforestation may get rid of them. Or it may be possible that a change of conditions will favour one of the local parasites and so bring about a new balance between the fly and its enemies. And by studying the precise habits of the creature, efficient methods of trapping may be devised.

That pests of this nature can cease to be serious is shown by the history of malaria and of plague. In various parts of Europe and America, these diseases, once serious, have wholly or virtually died out. And this has happened through a change in human environment and human habits. Take plague.

BIOLOGY AND PHYSICAL ENVIRONMENT

Modern man builds better houses, clears away more garbage, segregates cases of infectious diseases, is less tolerant of dirt and parasites, and in fine lives in such a way that his life is not in such close contact with that of rats. The result has been that rats have fewer chances of transmitting plague to man, and that the disease, if once transmitted, has less chance of spreading. With regard to malaria, although it is essential for quick results to utilize all the implications of Ross' and Grassi's great discovery that the disease is transmitted by mosquitoes, yet as a matter of history agricultural drainage, cleanliness and better general resistance, have, in many places, done as much or more than deliberate anti-mosquito campaigns to reduce or banish the disease.

So, too, typhus disappears with the spread of cleanliness, typhoid with the arrival of a good water supply ; and tuberculosis is more likely to be reduced by changed habits as regards fresh air, nourishing diet, and the public attitude to clean milk, than by any direct attack upon the tubercle bacillus.

WHAT DARE I THINK?

All the methods of which I have spoken have this in common—that they attempt to break the power of a pest by altering the rest of the environment, by directly or indirectly interfering with the balances of existing nature, so that the conditions shall no longer be so favourable for the obnoxious species.

But we could attack the problem from another angle. We could alter the very nature of Nature, changing the balance, not by changing the conditions, but by changing the inherent qualities of the organisms involved. For instance, instead of trying to attack a pest by means of introducing enemies, or altering the environment in which it has to carry on its operations, we can often deliberately breed stocks which shall be resistant to the attacks of the pest. Thus we can now produce relatively rust-proof wheat; and the Dutch have given us spectacular examples of what can be accomplished by the thoroughgoing application of Mendelian methods, by crossing a high-yielding but disease-susceptible sugar-cane with a related

BIOLOGY AND PHYSICAL ENVIRONMENT

wild species which is disease-resistant, and, in spite of the fact that the wild parent contains no trace of sugar, extracting from the cross after a few generations a disease-resistant plant with an exceptionally high yield of sugar.

Ecology here joins hands with genetics. And with genetics we may conclude our chapter, for it offers the prospect of the most radical transformations of our environment. Cows or sheep, rubber-plants or beets, represent from one aspect just so many living machines, designed to transform raw material into finished products available for man's use. And their machinery can be improved. Modern wheats yield several times as much per acre as the unimproved varieties grown by early and primitive agriculturists; and of late years, through the deliberate breeding of new types, the range of successful wheat cultivation has been extended nearly a hundred miles nearer the pole, and far into areas previously considered semi-desert.

Modern cows grow about twice as fast

as the cattle kept by primitive tribes; and when they are grown, produce two or three times as much milk in a year. This has thrown a new strain on the pastures upon which they feed, for the cow eventually draws its nourishment out of the soil, and if the animal machine for utilizing grass is improved, the plant machine which is responsible for the first stage of the process, of working up raw materials out of earth and air, must be improved correspondingly. Accordingly research is actively in progress not only to discover the best fertilizers for grass, but to manufacture new breeds of grass which shall be as much more efficient than ordinary grass as a modern dairy beast is than the aboriginal cow.

Of course, if we choose to give rein to our speculative fancy, there is hardly a limit to the goals to be set to deliberate breeding. Evolution is one long sermon on the text of the infinite plasticity of living matter. Temperament as well as anatomy, habits as well as structure, can be moulded by selection. We can breed out high-thyroid and low-

BIOLOGY AND PHYSICAL ENVIRONMENT

thyroid strains of doves, or tame and savage strains of rats, which depend on definite Mendelian differences as much as do blue-eyed or brown-eyed strains of human beings, or the tall and dwarf pea-plants of Mendel himself. If we wished, we could undoubtedly inflict upon other felines what we have already inflicted upon a number of breeds of domestic cat—namely, placid amiability in place of spitfire ferocity; and we could obtain tigers which, in actual fact, and not only in Mr Belloc's verse, were 'kittenish and mild.' But such speculations belong to the remoter future; and I leave my readers to pursue them in the pages of Mr Wells' *Men Like Gods* or Mr Stapledon's *First and Last Men*. They serve to remind us, however, in moments of discouragement in our more immediate and pedestrian tasks, of the possibilities that do exist, and of the folly of impatience in a world which achieves its real results not in tens but in thousands of years.

If I have chosen to concentrate largely upon the subject of pests, it is because it brings out so clearly the intricate inter-relationships of what we usually call the balance of nature, and the possibility of striking achievements, provided we build up the ecological science which alone can give us the necessary knowledge. There are plenty of other topics which could as fruitfully have been explored. Selective breeding I have just touched upon. I have hardly mentioned the sea, although it covers three-fifths of the earth's surface, and is inhabited in three dimensions instead of only two like the land. With the invention by Professor Hardy, of Hull, of the continuous plankton-recorder, we now can get a quantitative knowledge of the floating microscopic plants and animals that are at the basis of all the food-economics of the sea; with its aid we could and should prepare a map of the sea, analogous to a vegetation map of the earth, showing the zoning of the raw materials available for fish and whales, and of other larger and more humanly interesting life.

Then many microscopic forms of life themselves produce valuable materials : we could begin the deliberate cultivation of useful species of diatoms or filamentous algae or protophyta, with a view eventually to growing them on a large scale in enclosed bays or arms of the sea.

Again, now that Baly has been able to produce sugar (albeit only a trace) out of nothing but water, salts, air and light, we can look forward to steady progress in the direct synthesis of food-stuffs from inorganic matter. But progress is bound to be slow, and meanwhile we can set our existing methods in order by not wasting any of the essential raw materials used in nature's way of food manufacture by the agency of green plants. At the moment, the world is squandering its capital of available phosphorus and nitrogen certainly as fast as Great Britain is spending her accumulated financial capital. The chief way in which we waste it is by discharging our sewage into the sea, whence but little material ever returns to land. Nitrogen can be replaced out of the unlimited resources in the atmosphere, now that we have found how to tap those resources and turn them into available form. But there appears to be no reserve source of phosphorus : unless we want our descendants to starve, we must plan the conservation of this essential element.

These few examples must suffice to show the kind of control which man is just realizing he could exert over his environment. But they are enough to give us a new picture—the picture of a world controlled by man. It will never be fully controlled, for man cannot prevent earthquakes or eruptions, control the seasons or the length of day, change the climate of the Poles, stop hurricanes or ocean currents, or tap the resources of the ocean floor ; but just as the control exercised by man to-day is far greater than that exerted by any other animal species, so the future control of man will enormously exceed his present powers ; and even where he does not control, he will often, within limits, be regulating or guiding the course of nature ; and where he does not guide, he will at least be exploiting in a conscious and deliberate way.

BIOLOGY AND PHYSICAL ENVIRONMENT

The world will be parcelled out into what is needed for crops, what for forests, what for gardens and parks and games, what for the preservation of wild nature ; what grows on any part of the land's surface will grow there because of the conscious decision of man ; and many kinds of animals and plants will owe not merely the fact that they are allowed to grow and exist, but their characteristics and their very nature, to human control.

The sea will be mapped in new ways, exploited scientifically without waste, and much of it, almost certainly, will be farmed or cultivated as we cultivate the land, to give a larger yield. And disease-germs, pests, noxious weeds and vermin, will be in large measure abolished or, at least, under the thumb of a scientific humanity.

* * * * * *

But an organism is an interaction between the nature of its own protoplasm and the nature of its environment ; and to concentrate too exclusively upon the environment is to leave the greater half undone. In what follows, I must try to give some idea of the effect which biology may have upon human protoplasm, whether embodied in separate developing individuals or flowing onwards in the single evolutionary stream of the race.

CHAPTER II

Biology and the Human Individual

THE human individual is in certain important respects the most complicated bit of machinery in existence. And its machinery is, of course, biological. It is thus clearly impossible to survey the relations between biological science and the human organism in a single chapter; for to do this properly would require a treatise on physiology, a treatise on psychology, a treatise on embryology, and a treatise on medicine. All I can hope to do is, taking a great deal of knowledge for granted, to show some of the ways in which the advance of biological knowledge may be expected to react upon our attitude to our control of our individual human selves.

I do not want my readers to become angry with me at the outset. So, as I know what clouds of philosophic wrath can rise at the suggestion that man is a machine, I suppose I must devote a few words to justifying that harmless but necessary phrase.

Man is, from the external viewpoint of physical science, a bit of machinery. From another aspect, he is a spiritual being, whose emotional and intellectual activities, since they occur in the realm of consciousness and are non-spatial and non-material, are in a different order of existence. By some means, these two aspects are interdependent: it is the task of the future to determine precisely how. But this is irrelevant to our present point, which is, that in so far as man is made of matter—an indisputable if often inconvenient fact—he obeys the same laws as other material aggregations. The conservation of matter, the conservation of energy, the laws of chemical combination, the orderly sequence of events which we sum up as the principle of cause and effect—the progress of biology during the last hundred years has shown that these generalizations apply to an increasing number of aspects of living matter

BIOLOGY AND THE HUMAN INDIVIDUAL

as well as to matter which is not living, has enormously narrowed the field of life-processes in which they might possibly not hold, and has thrown the burden of proof that they may perhaps not be universally valid upon those who oppose this view. It is simply this applicability of the same laws to the same aspects, both of living and non-living matter, which I have in mind when I speak of an organism, human or otherwise, as a machine; and it is at least fair to say that it is not only the general working hypothesis of most biologists, but a working hypothesis which continues to justify itself by ever new fruits.

Most people at the word *machine* have a vision of something made of steel and utilizing the principles of mechanics to do its work. But you may have chemical machines or electrical machines. An electric cell is just as much a bit of machinery as a steam-hammer, a sulphuric acid plant just as much as a printing press. And the organism, though it contains machines which are purely mechanical in the classical sense, like the levers provided by the skeleton, is in the main a piece of chemical machinery, and, further, one whose chemistry is of an appalling order of complexity compared with most of the chemistry studied in ordinary chemical laboratories.

The working hypothesis of most biologists, then, is simply that man, like other organisms, has an aspect in which he can be studied and controlled as a piece of machinery —a very complicated piece of machinery, largely chemical, with great powers of self-regulation (they too dependent upon their own particular mechanisms) but none the less a piece of machinery. If they did not hold this working hypothesis, they would not be able to continue hoping for successful results from their work.

* * * * * *

During the last two centuries, and notably during the last seventy or eighty years, there has been a great deal of progress in understanding and controlling human machinery. But it has been limited in two main respects. It has been confined to the period after

BIOLOGY AND THE HUMAN INDIVIDUAL

birth, when the plasticity of the organism has been largely lost, and only minor changes can be induced ; and it has concerned itself, not unnaturally, much more with disease than with health, much more with remedying marked defects or departures from the normal, than in raising the normal to its optimum.

Let us consider these two aspects of the question : and first, the possibility of attacking and bringing under control that earlier and more astounding part of our life-history in which a human body is produced out of a tiny speck of protoplasm.

The human being, like other organisms, must develop : like other higher animals, he must develop from a fertilized egg—a mere single cell, microscopic in size and simple in structure. In his development, again like other animals, he passes through two main phases. There is an early phase, during which, without much growth, the main plan of the future human being is laid down, and a later phase, during which great growth occurs and details are filled in. During the first phase, development takes him from the state of a mere egg to that of a vertebrate, from a single spherical cell to an organism with head, brain, heart, digestive tube, limbs, skeleton, muscles, kidneys, and other necessary organs. During the second, the organs begin to work in their characteristic way, the mere vertebrate remoulds itself to fit itself for land life, reveals itself as a mammal, a primate, a human being; the ductless glands exert their action, and very considerable changes of proportion are brought about.

Now, in lower vertebrates, such as frogs, newts and fishes, in which the eggs are laid free in the water, biologists have found it possible to play a great many tricks upon development. They have been able to make a single egg produce twins or double monsters, either by mechanical constriction or by depriving it of oxygen at a certain critical stage. By exposing eggs to a temperature-gradient they have been able to make them grow into embryos with big heads and small tails, or vice versa, or with one lateral half of the body bigger than the other, according to

BIOLOGY AND THE HUMAN INDIVIDUAL

the direction of the gradient. They can reduce and even abolish the organs in the front of the head by exposing certain early stages of development to narcotics, and can exaggerate their size by stimulants. In frogs and trout, by delaying fertilization, they have been able to make eggs that ought to produce females, produce males instead (but, as they still contain the chromosomes of females, they can produce nothing but female offspring in the next generation).

All this is by treatment in the stages before definitive vertebrate ground-plan is laid down. But after this, all sorts of control are still possible. By the comparatively crude process of grafting, limbs and organs can be shifted from their proper positions, and made to grow almost anywhere the experimenter wishes. By exposing the young animal to different conditions, the functional response of its organs can be brought into play in very different ways: for instance, a young salamander can be made to produce gills several times as big and branched as normal by keeping it in poorly-aerated water, while its brother, kept in water artificially over-oxygenated, will have gills that are mere stumps.

By removing the animal's ductless glands at a very early stage, profound modifications of development can be made to occur. Tadpoles with either their thyroid or their pituitary removed will never turn into frogs; the presence of the pituitary seems to be necessary for the full development of the reproductive organs as well as for proper growth; and so on. Conversely, giving an excess of the secretion of this or that gland may have striking effects, and the earlier the treatment begins the more striking it will be. Young tadpoles given the right dose of thyroid will develop into frogs no bigger than house-flies, and with abnormally small limbs.

Then we are just beginning to know how to influence the rate of growth. Certain sulphur-containing compounds have been shown to stimulate growth in a marked way, and certain others to slow it down, the stimulating or retarding effect depending on whether the compounds are not or are oxi-

BIOLOGY AND THE HUMAN INDIVIDUAL

dized. What is especially interesting is that they appear to influence that sort of growth which depends upon the multiplication of cells, and not that which depends upon the cells' increase in size, so that by their use we ought to be able, not only to control growth in general, but to affect the growth of some organs more than others and so alter the animal's proportions.

This is all very interesting theoretically, but how could it be applied to organisms where, as in man, all the early and most susceptible stages of development are safely locked away in the mother's womb? Here, again, various possibilities suggest themselves. Many of my readers will remember how Mr Haldane in his *Daedalus* envisaged the possibility of 'ectogenesis,' or the bringing up of babies in incubators instead of in their mothers' bodies. We are a long way from realizing that possibility, and yet, in the short space of time since he wrote, the first step has been successfully taken. Professor Warren Lewis, of Baltimore, has succeeded in cultivating rabbits' eggs outside the body, from a moment immediately after fertilization to about a week later, when they have enlarged considerably and the embryo is showing the beginnings of organization. He has even recorded their development on the cinematograph; and it is one of the most astonishing spectacles to see, on the speeded-up film, the processes of cell-division, of organization, of growth, which have never before in any mammal taken place in the light of day, going on in the unfamiliar environment of a drop of nutrient fluid in a glass dish just as happily as in the dark recesses of the Fallopian tube, just as regularly as if the eggs were the eggs of sea-urchin or starfish in which development customarily takes place outside the body.

True, this is only the first step, and much harder ones remain to be taken; but if we reflect that it is not a century since the nature of fertilization and the mere external appearance of the early stages of development was discovered, it will be seen what progress biology has made.

If ectogenesis were ever possible, we could

play all the tricks we liked on the early development of man; and, as it is only during early development that there is the possibility of effecting any large alterations in the fundamental plan of the organism, its importance can be seen. For instance, the limit to human brain-power probably lies in the size of the female pelvis, which cannot give birth to babies with heads above a certain size. Abolish this cramping restriction, and you could embark upon an attempt to enlarge the human brain. Furthermore, as Haldane pointed out, ectogenesis would make it possible to practise an intensity and rapidity of eugenic selection enormously beyond what can be done if the human species keeps to its ancestral methods of development; but that is another story.

Then we must remember that much more of our growth takes place before birth than after. I shall be reminded that we weigh about seven pounds at birth, and perhaps a hundred and fifty at maturity. But growth is essentially a process of self-multiplication, so that the measure of growth is the number of times a piece of living substance multiplies itself. And, judged by this criterion, the pre-natal period is vastly more important. For the fertilized egg weighs about one-hundredth of a milligram, so that the baby at birth is about three hundred million times as large as when it began its independent career, while after birth it will only multiply itself about twenty times. Even from the time when the general plan is well established, the multiplication before birth is round about a million times.

Now this is important when we are considering changes of proportion. Changes of proportion are brought about owing to different parts or organs possessing slightly different rates of growth. In just the same way, two sums of money increasing at different rates of compound interest will be continually changing their proportionate amounts. The legs, for instance, grow a little faster than the trunk, the head a little slower. If we could find a means of altering the growth-rate of an organ, even by the merest fraction, during the whole of the prenatal period, we should make a big difference in the proportions of the resulting body. We are beginning to understand a little about the factors controlling the growth of parts relative to each other, and may perhaps be allowed to toy with the idea of controlling the process, producing at will stocky and thick-set fellows or leaner types with long legs and a long reach. And this, as well as other interferences with normal development, might well be possible, even if we could not cultivate the embryo outside the body, by means of injections.

Such speculations are worth thinking over; they seem far less unlikely candidates for realization within a century than would have appeared some of the modern applications of physico-chemical science, such as beam wireless, or million-volt transformers, or synthetic dyestuffs, to the physicists and chemists of a hundred years ago. However, there are other possibilities more nearly within our grasp, of which it is perhaps more profitable to speak; and here we shall see very clearly the restriction of earlier work to the medical side and to the rectification of defect.

Everybody to-day knows of the existence of the ductless glands. Indeed, the layman's idea of their powers is often exaggerated. Popular writers on science have been apt to let their enthusiasm run away with them, and imply that 'glands' are all-important—that the construction of the brain counts for much less in regard to personality than does the balance of the ductless glands, that they are omnipotent as far as the chemical regulation of the body is concerned, or that changes in the degree of their activity will account for a large part of vertebrate evolution.

But, even if we discount such one-sidedness, there is no doubt that they are of the greatest significance in the life of ourselves and other backboned animals. From one aspect they represent what we may call the chemical skeleton of the animal, each gland producing the same kind of stuff throughout its evolutionary career, whether in fish, frog, bird or human being. From another, some of them at least can be looked on as nature's drugs,

BIOLOGY AND THE HUMAN INDIVIDUAL

capable of whipping up the activities of ordinary flesh to otherwise unattainable heights, and yet without evil after-effects. Remove the human thyroid, for instance, and the general chemical activity of the body is cut down by about half. The thyroid hormone, as has aptly been said, is to the slow fire of living metabolism what a forced draught is to a furnace. The adrenal can discharge into the blood a substance which energizes the whole organism for emergencies. The hormone of the reproductive organs can sensitize the brain so that its activities are concentrated upon the opposite sex, and all else falls into a secondary place: in some cases even food is forgotten—the bull sea-elephant during the rut will go for weeks without once eating.

And every ductless gland has important functions to perform. The pituitary controls obesity, is concerned with gingering up placidity and sleepiness of temperament, promotes growth of the skeleton, is needed for the development of thyroid and reproductive organs. The thyroid is necessary for the development of normal brain-power and normal stature, and, in addition to its general function of forced draught, regulates the scale of temperament from sluggish to nervously excitable. The adrenal is concerned with the normal course of sexual development, and is responsible, it appears, for much of the general tone of the body as well as for the emergency energizing of which we have already spoken. The pancreas enables our tissues to utilize carbohydrate food; the parathyroid helps them to utilize lime, and probably keeps growth in check, while its deficiency induces one kind of tetany. The reproductive organs are responsible for the physical and mental differences between the sexes, as well as for the urge to love.

Thus most, and perhaps all of them, exert an effect upon, or perhaps we should say make a contribution to temperament, and many of them influence the proportions of the body.

Physique and temperament—here are the arcana of individuality. It would be natural to suppose that biological science would have exploited to the full the possibility of control disclosed by its discoveries concerning the ductless glands, and would be capable of moulding the individual to its will; yet this is very far from being the case. The knowledge has been used practically, but almost solely in the medical field. The control practised has been almost exclusively the control of markedly abnormal conditions. Insulin is given to correct diabetes: cretins may be restored to normality by thyroid treatment; grafts and extracts of the reproductive glands have been used successfully in under-sexed cases and in precocious senility; parathyroid helps in certain defective states of bones or teeth; and so on and so forth. These uses of our knowledge are important; they have saved many lives, rescued many people from ill-health. Yet the larger field remains almost untouched. Various pathological extremes of temperament, like those of a nervous, pop-eyed sufferer from Graves' Disease or of the Fat Boy in *Pickwick*, are known to be due to disturbances of ductless gland function; and so are various physiological extremes of physique, like the long-limbed giant, the heavy-faced and large-handed and large-footed acromegalic, the type who will put on vast quantities of flesh whatever his diet (the Fat Boy again), or the Peter Pan type of semi-dwarf who, though perfectly proportioned, never grows up fully.

It is further quite certain that differences of temperament and proportion which fall within the normal range are also in large measure due to differences in the balance of these same glands. What we are pleased to call the normal, however, includes a great many conditions which we regret. Poor general tone, hyper-sensibility, precocious obesity, premature ageing, growth which while stunted or over-lanky can hardly be called abnormal, undue shortness of arms and legs, unreflective energy and impetuosity that can hardly be called maniac but are always leading its possessor into awkward situations, placidity that oversteps the mark and becomes downright and cowlike dullness —there is no doubt that such endowments are more often than not due to some unusual con-

BIOLOGY AND THE HUMAN INDIVIDUAL

dition of the ductless glands. Would it not be admirable if we were in a position to remedy such flaws? would it not be convenient if we were able to adjust our temperament—within reason—to our circumstances?

Why then has so little been accomplished in this field? For one thing, because our knowledge is so recent. We must not forget that almost all the real advances in the study of the ductless glands date only from the present century, though fundamental pioneer work was accomplished about fifty years ago; the very word *hormone* is not thirty years old. Secondly, because in most cases the spur to discovery has first been applied by medicine : diseased conditions demanded cure, and the cause was found to reside in the defectiveness of this or that gland. But mainly because the subject is so complex. The earlier work in this field established the fact that each gland had some definite function : we could think of the thyroid doing this and the pituitary doing that, in the same clear-cut way, it seemed, as one could think of the cranium protecting the brain or the heart pumping the blood. But later work has shown that this picture is a gross over-simplification. Each gland does have a definite main function; but it can only exert that function by virtue of what other glands are doing or have previously done, and by its own function it is always modifying the working of its fellow-glands. The system of the ductless glands is, in fact, in a condition of elaborate balance; it constitutes, as one writer has well put it, an interlocking directorate.

The thyroid will not develop unless the pituitary is present; and, even when it is properly formed, its activity depends in part upon pituitary secretion. In the same way the reproductive glands need the secretion of the adrenal and of the pituitary if they are to grow normally. The pituitary gland consists of two quite distinct parts; and in lower animals, at least, the action of their two secretions is in certain aspects antagonistic. Excess of adrenal secretion causes the thyroid to damp down its activities. The different glands, in fact, are in a state of delicate equilibrium. The secretion of one stimulates the activity of a second, depresses that of a third, is activated by a fourth, and inhibited by a fifth; each change which is induced reverberates by action and reaction through the whole system.

The complexity of this arrangement has only fully dawned upon physiology in the last ten or fifteen years; several decades of hard work and patient exploration must elapse before the invisible machinery, the levers, springs, compensations and adjustments of this balanced system are fully understood. And we must set ourselves also to understand its variations. It is easy to see how a gross defect in one of its members will call forth serious symptoms, as when the pancreas is overworked, or the thyroid fails congenitally to develop. But, in a partnership so nicely adjusted and balanced, it is at the moment hard to understand just what underlies those quantitative alterations whose effects on temperament and physique remain within the bounds of the normal. The normal thyroid, for instance, has astonishing powers of adjusting its size and its activities to the calls upon it; what then determines that some people strike a balance with a slight over-activity of thyroid, others with a slight under-activity?

But it must be possible to find answers to these questions; and once the answers have been found, hitherto undreamt-of possibilities open out—of control over the very essence of our selves, over both physical and mental aspects of our organism.

The same sort of possibilities lie before the study of drugs. They, too, have in the past been used mainly for therapeutic purposes, to remedy definite defects of working in the bodily machine—to spur a flagging heart, to kill the germs of this or that disease, to stop bleeding, to induce anæsthesia, to promote the muscular contraction of the uterus in labour, to dull over-excited nerves, and so on. But, with rare exceptions, such as caffeine and alcohol, nicotine and cocaine, they find no place in everyday life; and of those which are so used, many are definitely harmful, and the rest can easily be abused.

Meanwhile the explorations of pharmaco-

BIOLOGY AND THE HUMAN INDIVIDUAL

logy are discovering many remarkable effects of chemical substances. Out of coal the pharmacologist can prepare acetanilide which will bring down the temperature; with other substances he can send the temperature up. Out of raw liver he gets a substance which will build blood; out of a Mexican cactus he can extract a drug which will promote the strength of visual imagery in thinking and will make some people hallucinate; he can manufacture out of ordinary materials in his laboratory the thyroxin with which the thyroid gland stimulates the body to new activity; he can reduce or increase the blood pressure at will. But, again, the results have been applied almost solely to set right something which has gone wrong, not to open new doors.

The fact seems to be that most of us are loath to consider this possibility of opening new doors, for the reason that those drugs which are now used deliberately for that purpose, like opium, alcohol or cocaine, are so readily abused. It seems a new garden on to which their doors open; but it has a way of turning into a prison. On the other hand, the very existence of the ductless glands reminds us that nature is drugging us every day without ill effects. A man whose thyroid has become defective must take a perfectly definite amount of thyroid extract every day if he is to remain in health : too little, and he still is sluggish in mind and body—too much, and he becomes thin and excitable. He cannot dispense with it any more than he can dispense with food ; but, whereas normally he should make it for himself, now he has to be provided with it from the outside. And, again, as with food, both too much and too little are harmful.

It should not be impossible to work out a combination of pharmacological substances, each in the right amount and right proportion, which would be capable of toning up a man's faculties by say ten per cent., and yet having no bad after-effect, other than what is already exerted by our nervous, rushing modern lives. It would be somewhat different according to the kind of work which was needed—hard physical labour like that of a

BIOLOGY AND THE HUMAN INDIVIDUAL

miner, unremitting activity of various sorts like that of a cabinet minister, routine like that of a civil servant, pure brain-work like that of a mathematician; and as our knowledge is increased, the prescription could be adjusted to individual physique and temperament.

At the end of Jules Romains' play, *Dr Knock*, the doctor expatiates on the glories he has achieved for medicine, by persuading vast numbers of perfectly well people that they are ill. With a wave of his hand, he reminds his hearers that at this very moment, within sight of his house, five thousand gullets are swallowing their evening potion, and in a moment five thousand temperatures will be taken. It would be an even greater triumph for medicine if it could invent something which would make the average well man feel better, and persuade the population at large to adopt it, so that not thousands but millions would simultaneously be taking their 'little daily dose.'

And then there is the psychological side of biology. Pure human psychology is at the moment a somewhat isolated and esoteric science. But it cannot long stay in this position. Accurate studies on the brain, such as those of the great Pavlov, are linking it with nerve-physiology. Work such as that of Kretschmer and Draper is joining it up with general physiology and is emphasizing from another angle the unity of mind and matter within the single organism. The vast amount of recent work on animal behaviour which at last of late years has paid serious attention to the monkeys and apes as well as to cats, pigeons, frogs, ants and worms, is providing the proper evolutionary background; by so doing, if it may rob human psychology of some of its more romantic speculations, it will force it into biological sanity.

Already many new possibilities are opening up. There is the possibility that we may be able to bring children up without the deformation of fear, the friction and waste engendered by repression, the abnormal preoccupation with sex, which have in the past hindered the free use of the energy of human minds. We are just beginning to see that the

BIOLOGY AND THE HUMAN INDIVIDUAL

rule-of-thumb methods of our ancestors might be replaced by a scientific cultivation of the mind, the one as different from the other as is modern scientific agriculture from the shifting cultivation of a primitive tribe.

We can see the possibility; but as yet we can hardly envisage the result. What changes in conditions of work would be demanded by a population bursting with mental energy? What alterations in marriage and sexual relations in general would result from an uninhibited mental attitude towards sex? What would be the result upon our political system of an all-round enlargement of rationality and freedom?

It is impossible to say; but it is clear that the most exciting and, indeed, disturbing possibilities loom up before a civilization equipped with the psychological knowledge which will inevitably have been gained before the end of the present century—the possibility of training the mental organism in new forms, and of tapping new supplies of mental energy in the life of the population as a whole.

*   *   *   *   *   *

WHAT DARE I THINK?

I might have multiplied examples, especially from medicine; I might have spoken of the very real possibilities of prolonging life —so-called 'rejuvenation'—opened up by various operations on ductless glands. But I have, I hope, said enough for my purpose. My purpose was simply this: to show that biology is entering upon the phase begun by physico-chemical science about a century ago, where knowledge can be translated on a large scale into practical control. This new practical control will in many respects have more fundamental effects than the old, since it will be exerting its influence not on the nature around man, but upon man himself. The prospect is disturbing, in some ways perhaps even alarming. But that is all the more reason for facing it in time and in the right spirit. There will be no preventing its coming, no possibility of holding back the tide. But we can prevent its advance being piecemeal and haphazard, and can use our imaginations ahead of the event. The difficulty with the applications of science has often been that they acquire a momentum of their own and take charge of events. Samuel Butler envisaged industrial humanity as the servants, slaves or parasites of the machines which represent the latest dominant type of existence brought forth by evolution ; and there is something in what he said. Man as scientist can provide practical control of phenomena. It is for man as man to control that control.

CHAPTER III

Man and his Heredity

AT the instant of our conception, we are dealt the hand of cards with which we have, willy-nilly, to play the game of life; what hand we shall get at this inevitable moment is almost as much a matter of mere chance as it is each of the trivial times when we pick up the thirteen bits of pasteboard from the green baize of the card table. That is one of the twentieth-century discoveries of biology; if you prefer, it is an amplification of what was in some measure known before. But the amplification is so radical that it does really constitute a new discovery; for it substitutes for the vague guesses of earlier generations the picture of a precise and orderly mechanism, for loose and general ideas a detailed and accurate scientific theory. It is no exaggeration to say that in the thirty years of the present century heredity has risen from one of the vaguest and most backward of the biological subsciences to become the discipline in which biology most nearly approximates to the type of physics, pattern of the natural sciences, in which induction, theory, deduction and experimental testing play equal and complementary rôles in an indivisible and rapidly advancing whole.

Let us return to that moment of destiny when our inheritance is decided. How fantastic is the scene of the microscopic drama, how alien from the ideas of other ages the ideas which it paints on the background of our thought ! There is no generation of life by the masculine principle in a mere soil provided by the female ; there is no breathing in of wholly new life from supernatural or, indeed, any external agency. It is not the mother's blood which decides the temperament and capacities of the child, nor what she and still less the father have eaten, drunk, experienced or thought about. There is a continuity of life and living matter both from the father and the mother to the offspring :

two fragments of living matter, which have detached themselves from the parental bodies, unite to form the one fragment which will grow into the body of the child; and the child's qualities are determined, in so far as heredity has its say in the matter, by the particular assortment of chemical units which it receives at this instant.

One inert spherical piece of living matter, somewhere about a hundredth of a cubic millimetre in bulk, just visible under a hand-lens, has been squirted by hydraulic pressure out of the water-cushion in which it has grown to maturity in the little pinkish warty ovary. Wrapped round by the frilled trumpet mouth of the tube which leads from the central cavity of the body to the outer world, it is forced downwards into the dark and corrugated recesses of the duct. There, because two human beings, a man and a woman, have been led by love or driven by lust, it finds itself in the presence of some members of a huge population, as great as the entire human population of London or New York, of strange and altogether microscopic creatures, the sperms, which resemble miniature, more active, but less intelligent tadpoles—lashing their tails, being swirled blindly hither and thither by the currents—all but imperceptible to us, violent to them—which the tube engenders in the fluid cavity by means of microscopic hairs ranged upon its walls.

These also are members of the human race, for the discoveries of the nineteenth century concerning reproduction have shown that we, like all higher animals, consist (as Professor Punnett has pithily put it) not of two kinds of individuals, but four. In addition to the familiar large human individuals, men and women, there are the much more abundant, simpler and tinier human individuals, the male and female gametes or reproductive cells. In ourselves, the life of these little people is short; but in lower creatures, fish or sea-urchins or worms, it is both longer and more independent, for they swim or float around and meet their fate in the open waters of the sea. In the highest types, however, this independence has been abolished; they never see the light of day, but live their little lives entirely within the bodies of the other kinds of individual.

But to return to the blind hand of hereditary destiny. No two of these swarming millions are alike. Let me explain. I began by comparing our hereditary destiny with a hand of cards. That is correct as far as it goes, but the system is more complicated than in any human card game. The cards of physical heredity are tiny submicroscopic particles called *genes*. Every one of us has two complete packs of these hereditary cards in every cell of our bodies, one pack derived from our father, one from our mother. But, instead of a pack containing fifty-two cards only, it contains several hundreds, perhaps even thousands. And each kind of card can exist in a number of forms : it is as if a Jack of Hearts, for instance, were not always just a Jack of Hearts, but could be a Jack of Hearts one stage above par, so to speak ; or two stages above par ; or one, two, three stages below par ; or even in a form that differed a little in quality as well as quantity from the standard. The different forms have all been derived by sudden chemical change or mutation from the original form, and reproduce themselves true to type so long as a further mutation does not strike them and change them further.

Now, when the time comes for the formation of the little people from the big people, the reproductive sperms and eggs from the men and women, the double packs are sorted out into single packs, and each reproductive cell gets one single but complete pack. The sorting, however, is of such a nature that it is in the highest degree improbable that it will ever be done twice in exactly the same way. Each reproductive cell receives a whole pack, but within this the proportion of hereditary cards which came from the mother and those which came from the father will never twice be the same.

In the case of the sperms, the process is such that, after the separation into single packs, each kind of single pack is allotted not to one but to two sperms. So that it is not strictly true to say that no two are alike; the sperms exist in the form of innumerable pairs of identical twins; and no two of the pairs are alike in the hereditary outfit which they carry. In man, normally only one egg is formed at a time; but it has received a single gene-pack, and the precise composition of this is again a matter of chance.

Thus the interest of the strange scene deepens. Egg and sperms carry the destiny of the generations. The egg realizes one chance combination out of an infinity of possibilities: and it is confronted with millions of pairs of sperms, each one actually different in the combination of cards which it holds.

Then comes the final moment in the drama—the marriage of egg and sperm to produce the beginning of a large individual. One sperm penetrates the egg, fuses entirely with it, and the two single packs of gene-cards are mingled to form one new double pack—the new human being's hereditary destiny. Once a single sperm has penetrated the microscopic skin of the egg, all the others are destined to a sterile death: for at this instant a change takes place in the egg, barring the entry of any further sperms. And the marriage is absolute; there is no divorce.

Here, too, it seems to be entirely a matter of chance which particular union of all the millions of possible unions shall be consummated. One might have produced a genius, another a moron; a third would have given a robust giant, a fourth an inevitable weakling; half must automatically give rise to boys, the other half equally automatically to girls; and so on. But which of all the possibilities shall actually be realized is determined by the accident of which sperm is first swirled up to the egg and can stay there long enough to burrow its pointed nose into its partner's transparent flesh.

With a realization of all that this implies, we can banish from human thought a host of fears and superstitions. No basis now remains for any doctrine of metempsychosis; for the belief that maternal impressions or meditations can determine the character or appearance of the unborn child; for the notion that life is not continuous, but at some specified moment created anew in each generation; for the host of beliefs which maintain that sex is determined mainly or wholly by diet or other agencies acting after conception. The ground is cleared for the new and scientific doctrine of genetic destiny—a destiny inevitable so far as it goes, but elastic within wide limits in its realization.

Let us look a little further into the implications of this last sentence.

The biologist is often asked: Which is the more important, Heredity or Environment? and he cannot answer, for the simple reason that the question has no answer. Neither is more important, because both are essential. The organism at any moment, be it embryo or foetus, child or man, is the result of an interaction of the particular heredity which it has received with the particular environment in which it has grown up : or, since there is only one hereditary outfit to be considered, but an infinity of possible environments, we may say that there is an infinity of possible expressions of the one heredity, and that the actual organism is that one particular expression which has been evolved by that one particular environment to which it has been exposed.

So the question which could rightly be asked of the biologist is this: Granted that we are confronted with two different organisms—men, or cats, or wheat-plants—then is the *difference* between them due wholly or mainly to a difference in their hereditary outfits, or wholly or mainly to a difference in their environments during development? And that question *can* be answered. It can never be answered offhand, but it is at least capable of being answered if we can lay our hands on the right information.

So that, strictly speaking, no character is purely hereditary. We usually say that the colour of the eyes in man is purely hereditary: we mean that, granted a normal prenatal environment which permits of a normal human baby being born, the difference between blue and brown eyes is due entirely to a difference in hereditary outfit. But we must not forget that in certain circumstances an embryo may develop which has no eyes at all, though it possesses the genes which in more favourable conditions would have given rise to the eyes; and, doubtless, if we could alter slightly the conditions in the womb, we should be able to make babies that ought to be blue-eyed grow brown eyes, or vice versa. So let us never forget that the individual man or woman is always one of many possible expressions of a particular heredity reacting with one of many possible environments, just as the result of a rubber of bridge is due to an interaction between the hands dealt with the play of the four players. Or, again, the inheritance is like the seed, the environment like the soil; and the organism is like the resultant plant.

Clearly these facts are full of implications alike for our philosophical outlook and our practical statesmanship. But before we need worry our heads over the subtleties of genetic difference, we are confronted by the simpler racial problem of mere quantity—the regulation of population, both on a national and a world-wide scale. Humanity is so used to individualism in this matter that not even

Communistic Russia or Fascist Italy has yet envisaged any but the most indirect means of attacking the problem. So that the first thing to accomplish is to get accustomed to the idea that it can be attacked directly. For instance, in the present economic crisis where over-production grimly faces under-employment, plenty of remedies have been proposed which envisage adjusting economic processes like production to population; but, so far as I am aware, not one responsible person has even suggested that the reverse procedure may be equally necessary: in other words, that without also beginning deliberately to adjust population to economic processes, the problem will never be solved. The only moves in that direction have been the restrictions proposed upon immigration; but these by themselves will be quite negligible in their effects.

But how *could* one even attempt the direct control of quantity of population? That doubtless is what the ordinary intelligent man or woman of to-day will exclaim. It would be an impossible interference with individual liberty, an unwarranted tampering with a sacred function! The answer to this is simple—cease looking at the problem from inside the narrow circle of the ordinary ideas of your time; get outside yourself into the spaciousness of history and the liberty of pure reasonableness, and you will see that neither objection has any necessary validity. Things are sacred because we think them sacred; and, in any case, sanctity is no argument against deliberate political control, as witness the numerous national churches, or the State regulation of marriage. Innumerable sanctities have had the tabu taken out of them and been subjected to reasonable regulation, and yet have not ceased to possess their essential sacredness. As for liberty, what greater infringement of personal liberty can there be than conscription of individual men for war? and if over- or under-population is a danger to the national fabric, why not conscription of reproduction for peace? Before the nature of infectious diseases was understood, the regulations in force to-day as to notification, quarantine, and so forth would have been regarded as gross infringements of personal liberty : compulsory education was by many people regarded in the same light. So, as the processes of population-growth and their effects are better understood and realized, we shall cease to regard them as mysteries beyond our interference, but see in them yet another field which the labours of knowledge have made ripe for the harvest of rational control.

A simple method for exerting some control over population-growth, which could be introduced as soon as the obvious course has been taken of making birth-control information freely available to all, would be to link it on to public relief. A married man, whether through his own fault or that of economic forces beyond his control, is being supported wholly or mainly out of public funds. The State may fairly be asked to see that neither he nor his family shall starve ; but it may fairly ask in return that he shall not increase the load to be carried, by increasing the size of his family. Continuance of relief could quite easily be made conditional upon his having no more children. Infringement of this order could probably be met by a short period of segregation, say in a labour camp. After three or six months' separation from his wife he would be likely to be more careful next time. Sterilization has been suggested, but this seems disproportionate save in recidivist cases of philoprogenitiveness which seem otherwise incurable.

As a matter of fact, although at the moment the need for restriction of births seems the more urgent in crowded countries like our own, it is more than likely that the opposite need may in a comparatively short time prove the more serious. Let us take an example. In Great Britain the population is still increasing at the rate of over 200,000 per annum. But this increase is, biologically speaking, illusory. It is a mere after-effect of the fact that the grandparents of the young people of to-day had a much higher birth-rate than have their parents. Accordingly the grandparents produced a large crop of human beings of reproductive age in the next generation. But the next crop has been far smaller; so that when it in its turn comes to reproductive age, it will, except in the purely supposititious and very unlikely event of their changing their reproductive habits and having much larger families than their parents, give rise to a much smaller absolute crop of babies. In other words, it takes at least two generations for a fall in the birth-rate to exert its full effect. It has an immediate effect in lowering the number of babies born; and an even more important effect in lowering the number of prospective parents for the next generation.

Or we can look at the matter in another way. The present rate of increase would not exist if, simultaneously with the fall in the birth-rate, there had not been a general fall in the death-rate. In other words, fewer babies are born, but proportionately more of them survive to maturity and old age. The effect of this, which will be shown markedly about twenty years hence, is that the composition of the population is changing: it is coming to consist more of old people, less of young people. But we must all die some time.

WHAT DARE I THINK?

So that as the average age of the population goes up, an automatic increase of the death-rate will set in. This is the chief reason why the death-rate in France is so much higher than in England, while the birth-rate is about the same. It is not so much that France's population does not increase because of its high death-rate, as that it shows a high death-rate because it has not been increasing appreciably for a couple of generations.

And, finally, this leads on to another consideration. During the last half century birth-rate and death-rate have pretty well kept pace with each other in their fall. But there is a fundamental difference between them; for whereas the death-rate cannot fall below a certain quite appreciable figure, the birth-rate could conceivably fall to zero. Concretely, while we cannot expect any large reduction in the death-rate during the remainder of the present century, it is perfectly possible and even likely that the birth-rate may continue its downward career. Cinemas, motor-cars, cheap luxuries, travel, the general cult of having a good time—these all compete either financially or psychologically with children. The more we equalize opportunity, the more facilities for enjoyment or self-development our civilization provides to the economically lower strata of society, the fewer children are they likely to have. And as it is these classes alone which at the present moment are producing enough children to reproduce themselves, the effect will be marked.

The net result of what I have been saying is this. That, even if the present birth- and death-rates remain unchanged, the population of Great Britain will be declining in twenty years' time. But we have every reason to suppose that the birth-rate will fall much faster than the death-rate, so that the decline will probably begin earlier and proceed more rapidly. Approximately the same is true for other Western European nations such as Germany; and even the United States, according to that eminent statistician Dr Dublin, will see its downward turning-point about 1970.

Then, of course, there will be a hullabaloo,

and we shall hear much wild talk about decadence, the collapse of Western civilization, race-suicide, and the like. The question will, however, remain—what is to be done about it? Propaganda, of the right sort, may exert a real influence on the public mind. But as the reasons for small families are largely economic, we must look to economic agencies for a large part of what correction may be necessary. Bonuses for very large families will accomplish next to nothing, because large families are rare phenomena, and the agencies at work are universal or, at least, general. We shall, therefore, have to have recourse to some form of family allowance scheme, designed with definite biological ends in view. But as family allowance schemes must take quality as well as quantity into account, I will leave their consideration until later.

A more difficult, though also a more exciting, set of problems confronts us when we come to think of the quality of population—in other words, when we begin to be Eugenists.

It is convenient to pigeonhole our ideas, and the usual way of pigeonholing our ideas on eugenics is to divide the subject into negative and positive. Negative eugenics is concerned with preventing degeneration, while positive eugenics aims at the improvement of the human stock. Perhaps a better method of classification is to divide the subject into short-range and long-range eugenics. Short-range eugenics concerns itself merely with altering the proportions of already existing and commonly recurring human types within the total population, while long-range eugenics sets itself the aim of bringing new types into existence. And both of these, of course, have their positive and their negative sides.

I said that short-range eugenics aimed *merely* at altering the proportions of existing kinds of human beings. That *merely* must be taken in relation to the much larger aims of long-range eugenics, and to the slow and enormous processes of Evolution in general. In relation to human history (itself so far a short-range process, biologically considered), short-range eugenics is of utmost importance, and may well turn out to be the most urgent human problem of the next few centuries. For do not let us forget that the human race consists of an astounding variety and range of different kinds of men. From savage to Nordic business man, from hunting pigmy to Chinese sage, the race is prodigal in types ; and even within the single race or nation we range from imbecile and moron to man of talent or genius, from those congenitally weak and susceptible to disease to those born to be champion athletes, those who through inheritance lack moral or aesthetic feeling to those hypersensitive to virtue or to beauty. And even when we have made all allowances for environment and upbringing, the major part of these differences in type is due to differences in inborn constitutions. Even if we leave the rare extremes out of account, the monsters and the idiots, the hypersensitives and geniuses, any reshuffling of the proportions of the types that are left will be important enough. It matters a great deal whether one quarter or three quarters of the community shall have their brains of poor quality or of good quality; whether the proportion of those endowed by nature with initiative be halved or doubled; whether, when we have made England a home fit for heroes to live in, we shall find that there are fewer heroes and more human sheep to inhabit it; whether congenital debility and defect goes up or down.

Let us take the case of mental defect in illustration. I am using the term mentally defective in its strict sense, of some one with such a feeble mind that he cannot support himself or look after himself unaided, and not in the loose sense which would include the much larger class of borderline types generally called morons by American writers. The number of such mentally defective persons in Great Britain is now over 300,000, according to a very careful Government Report published in 1929; in other words, one in every hundred-and-twenty of our population is through sheer insufficiency of brains incapable of pulling his weight in the national life; and this, of course, leaves on one side all those incapable on account of insanity or of purely physical handicap.

That is bad enough. But there is worse behind it. Another committee reported on the same subject twenty-five years previously, and it found a far lower proportion of mental defectives.[1] We are making two mental defectives grow where only one grew before.

The only plausible reason advanced for this state of affairs is that it is an effect of the improvement in our measures of public health and preventive medicine, especially with regard to infant welfare. Mentally defective children are on the average less resistant in other ways; and their usual upbringing leaves more to be desired than that of normal children. Accordingly, if our infant welfare schemes save a thousand babies which other-

[1] It may be objected that the increase from then till now might be only apparent, due to a greater ease in the ascertainment of defect; the earlier committee simply missed a lot of defectives. But for a variety of technical reasons this appears quite definitely not to be the case. At its face value the increase in twenty-five years represents an actual doubling of the percentage of mental defectives. When all possible allowances have been made, the real increase, it would seem, must be considerable.

wise would have died, we are likely to save a disproportionate number of mentally defective children among them. Nine hundred and ninety of them may be fine babies, whose preservation is a national asset; but if the remaining ten are mental defectives, and if ten per thousand is a higher proportion of defectives than exists in the population at large, then we are increasing the percentage of defectives in the new generation. By reducing the rigour of natural selection, we are allowing an undue proportion of unfit types to survive. And, as in all probability, new hereditary variations towards defectiveness are more common than those towards an improvement of the type, there is no saying where such a process may end.

What is to be done about it? The purely biological method of keeping the stock up to standard by natural selection is, though effective, cruel and uneconomical. It involves wholesale destruction to make sure that the few types you want destroyed shall be included in the holocaust, thus showing a resemblance to Elia's account of the original method for obtaining roast pork. It is of the essence of civilization to set its face against such haphazard, blind and wasteful methods.

There is only one immediate thing to be done—to ensure that mental defectives shall not have children. Whether this should be achieved by the prohibition of marriage, or, as many believe, by combining the method of segregation in institutions with that of sterilization for those who are at large, is not our present concern. We want a general agreement that it is not in the interests of the present community, the race of the future, or the children who might be born to defectives, that defectives should beget offspring. When discussing concrete proposals, this simple question should always be in mind: 'Do you want mentally defective people to have children?'

If, by whatever means, defectives can be prevented from reproduction, then, since the considerable majority of mental defect is due to hereditary factors, it will decrease from generation to generation. The decrease will, unfortunately, not be very fast, since much hereditary defect is caused by what are known as recessive factors, which can be carried in a latent state by apparently normal people. When two such 'carriers' mate, they will produce a certain proportion of defective children. But, in spite of this, to prevent defectives themselves from having children would, in point of fact, steadily decrease the percentage of defectives in each generation.

The next step, could it only be achieved, would be to discover how to diagnose the carriers of defects. If these could but be detected, and then discouraged or prevented from reproduction, mental defect could very speedily be reduced to quite small proportions among our population. There is nothing inherently improbable in our being able to discover a test for carriers : but we have not done so yet, and have no very immediate prospect of doing so in the future.

There is, of course, a still further question : how the original defective genes which are responsible for inherited mental defect were produced in the first place. Of this we know next to nothing, save that they must, on analogy with hereditary defect in animals, have arisen as a sudden sport or mutation. We know, further, that mutations arise haphazard in a very small proportion of a population, and that X-rays seem to have something to do with their production.

But even if we knew just what caused the lamentable mutations that led to inherited mental defect, and even if we could go further and prevent any more such mutations from occurring, we should not be able by this means to do much towards the reduction of mental defect. For almost all the inherited mental defect in existence, and all the latent defect in the bodies of carriers, owes its existence to mutations which have taken place generations ago. The only way of effectively reducing inherited mental defect is to prevent the breeding of those who carry it, whether in visible or invisible form.

I have spent some time over this question, since it brings up the issues of short-range eugenics in clear-cut form. There is in process a change in the proportion of genetic type within our population: it is a regrettable change: we can give a reasonable explanation for it: and we can envisage practical measures for putting an end to the racial degeneration which it involves.

But a more penetrating prophecy of degeneration has recently been given by Dr R. A. Fisher,[1] whose mathematical talents, so long devoted to the analysis of experimental agriculture, are now fertilizing eugenics as well as the general theory of evolution.

His starting point is the celebrated observation made by Galton, that noble (or other) families whose representatives marry heiresses tend to die out with abnormal frequency. This fact Galton brilliantly explained by pointing out that the heiresses would not have been heiresses if they were not members of very small families, so that the probability was that they inherited, together with their wealth, a congenital tendency to low fertility. Thus two factors which are not of necessity interconnected, female wealth and low fertility, are automatically brought into conjunction.

[1] In *The Genetical Basis of Natural Selection* (Oxford Press, 1930).

Fisher has simply generalized this particular case, and applied the principle to society as a whole. He points out that in primitive societies, organized for efficiency in war, with polygamy as the recognized practice, the qualities which made for success would in general come to be coupled with an increased fertility. For prowess on the whole will lead to success, and success to more wives: while large families are not only honoured and applauded but, far from being an economic or social drag, are a help and a solace to their parents. But the historical change from tribal times, through an aristocratic period where wealth was based on land, to unrestricted commercialism or individualism, particularly since coupled with the change to monogamy, and particularly in its later stages when the world is filling up, has completely altered the picture. And Fisher lays down as a general law that in any society of our general economic type, the two biologically independent variables of those tendencies making for success and those making for low fertility, of social necessity become coupled together. And since these tendencies are largely genetic, the result is a progressive and cumulative diminution within the population of the proportion of gene-units making for success, and therefore of the successful type of person.

I speak of 'tendencies.' These may be of the most varied nature. The tendencies making for low fertility may be purely physiological, such as defects in the reproductive apparatus; they may be temperamental, like extreme caution; they may have a more complex psychological basis, as when ambition overrides desire for children. And the tendencies making for success may be pure intellect or mere energy, charm or ruthlessness, personal magnetism or literary genius. So long as there is any hereditary basis for these, the coupling of them together can have only one result—the decrease within the stock of the qualities which make for success. For of two business or professional men of equal brains and ability but different number of children, the one with the fewer children will usually be able to concentrate more on his work, to avoid more worries, to rise more rapidly; and, what is biologically even of greater importance, his children will receive a better education, more chances of travel and pleasure, a more favourable start in life, a greater financial inheritance at his death, and be able to contract marriages that socially and financially are more eligible. Conversely, of two men with the same-sized families, but of differing abilities, the one with more of the qualities making for success will usually rise the faster. And this applies throughout society in so far as society is commercial and individualistic. It will not apply of necessity to the lowest grades of unskilled labour; but as this stratum must presumably contain more than its due proportion of unsuccessful types who have slipped down the social ladder, and as families in this stratum are well above the average size, actually it provides no exception. The only notable exception concerns that type of agriculture in which the children can be usefully employed from an early age, and are therefore an asset; but this constitutes but a very small and a decreasing fraction of modern society.

Let us give two examples to point the moral. Most people would agree that men who have been educated at Harvard come from stock which is above the average of success in America. Now, if Harvard were to recruit itself entirely from the sons of its alumni, then, even if every Harvard man were compelled to send his sons to the old college, the institution would progressively and quite rapidly decline; for the average number of sons which Harvard alumni now have is not three or four, as it would have been in earlier ages, not even one, which is necessary to maintain the absolute numbers of Harvard-educated stock, but only about three-quarters.

The other example comes from England. In the census of 1911, the only one for which accurate figures on this subject are available, the population was grouped into five main economic classes, of which the highest included all the professional classes, as well as some others, while the lowest consisted of unskilled labour. This lowest economic class had a fertility which, even after all corrections were made for infant mortality, age of marriage and so forth, was not only about double that of the professional group, but was nearly fifty per cent. above that of the population as a whole. As a result, the economically least successful twenty per cent. of the working population existing in 1911 gave rise to about twenty-five per cent. of the next generation of Englishmen.

It is of course obvious that an unskilled labourer need not be genetically inferior to a member of the professional classes ; a dustman may be superior to a Duke in eugenic as in moral worth. But in so far as any ladder of opportunity exists, it provides a means whereby the better endowed may rise in the social-economic scale, the worse endowed may sink. This must bring about a certain difference in the average inherited endowment of the different strata : and in evolution it is average values which count.

Fisher further goes on to point out that, far from man being universally more exempt from natural selection than are wild species of animal or plant, in regard to one characteristic at least he is exceptionally subject to selective influences, and that is fertility. The reason for this is that human beings vary far more in regard to their actual fertility than do wild species of animals or plants. Lions may vary from, say, two to five in number of offspring, snowshoe rabbits from perhaps three to twelve; but human families range regularly from zero to ten, fifteen, or even twenty. The number of couples with two, one, or no children, is relatively large; and thus the possessors of six, five, or even four children, are at an enormous reproductive advantage. If this were all, then the quicker-multiplying stocks would simply increase at the expense of the slower, a process which we may observe in Eastern Canada to-day. But if other qualities, desirable or undesirable, come to be associated with fertility, then the automatic reproductive selection which fertility brings will change the stock in these regards as well. And the evolutionary changes thus effected can be, as Fisher points out, far more rapid than any evolutionary change brought about by selection in any non-human species.

What, then, is the effect of this coupling, which has come into being through the agency of our economic system, of the tendencies to failure and fertility? There are tender-minded people and liberal doctrinaires who will seriously argue that the qualities which make for success are, on balance, not particularly good, or even that they are evil. Ruthlessness, egotism, vulgarity, double-dealing, subservience, the limitations that are willing to concentrate on dull routine—all these only too often make for success, and it is a good thing that the race should be purged of them.

Granted; but we must not forget that brains, energy, concentration, special gifts, devotion to ideals—these too in general make for success. And most people would, I think, agree that this second list more than counterbalances the first; for even if vulgarity and ruthlessness and the rest are unpleasant, they can be combated; but without brains, energy, and special talents, the world would both collapse and cease to be worth living in. It is true that there is scriptural warrant for the view that the meek shall inherit the earth : and a tendency in that direction is one result of our modern civilization. But it is only one result ; the other tendencies are for the stupid to inherit the earth, and the shiftless, and the imprudent, and the dull. And this is a prospect neither scriptural nor attractive.

I for one regard the state of affairs as definitely gloomy. What, then, is the remedy for it? One is to alter your whole economic and social system ; but that, however desirable, could only be brought about so slowly that the cumulative dysgenic process would have had time to work a very great deal of harm before the remedy began to be effective. This may be the ultimate goal : but meanwhile we need some remedy which will work within the limits of our existing system.

R. A. Fisher himself suggests a comprehensive scheme of family allowances, not restricted to the labouring classes, but running right through society; not all on the same scale, but with the amount per child proportional to the man's total or at least to his earned income. The extension throughout society is necessary if the progressive reduction in the numbers of the best-trained, most intelligent, and most successful stocks is to be checked. By the same token, the second proviso is also necessary. A contribution per child which would mean a great deal to an unskilled labourer, would be trifling to a professional man, while the really successful would not even find it worth while to fill in the necessary forms. The proviso has the additional merit that it is elastic: if the economic system changes so that the manual workers receive more, the manufacturer or organizer less, their family allowances will go up or down to suit the new scale.

At first sight, such a scheme may appear unjust and undemocratic, pushing to extreme lengths the principle of giving to those who already have. But if we look at it in its true light, the injustice is seen to be apparent only. The scheme is simply intended to remedy the existing economic disadvantages of having children : it is an adjustment of wages or salaries to the conditions of family life. Under our present economic system, we pay different amounts to different groups of people : one group, say, gets two hundred pounds a year, another group two thousand. In each group, the man with children is being economically handicapped, while the childless man is for all practical purposes receiving a bonus for his childlessness. The suggested scheme of family allowances is merely intended as a biological measure, designed to equalize matters within each group, by correcting wages or salary for number of children. If society decrees that the poorer classes shall be better paid, or that the richer shall get less, the correction automatically follows suit. But it is a correction which has to be applied for biological reasons, and in applying it we must accept economic facts as we find them.

For the wage-earning classes, the system of wage-pools, already successfully adopted as the basis of the widespread system of family allowance in vigour in France, would be satisfactory; and a similar method could be applied to many of the professional classes. With those who draw money from many sources, like doctors, it would be more difficult to devise a scheme which could be put into immediate operation; but once the principle had been agreed on, its general application could be slowly but surely worked out.

It is difficult to see any other measure which would have any marked effect on this degenerative tendency, apart from radical change in economic system, as in Russia, or equally radical change in social system, involving State charge of children; and even with such a comprehensive scheme of family allowances, it is difficult to believe that the process would be wholly checked, for there are intangible factors at work, such as the desire to be free to travel, to write or do research, as well as merely financial considerations, operating to restrict the size of families of successful people; and there will remain the temptation to marry money, and with it bring low fertility into the family. All one can say is that such a measure, combined with similar measures such as free (and good) higher education for all, would undoubtedly help to check a process which, if left to itself, would inevitably cause the collapse of our civilization, and to give us a breathing space in which to look for other weapons to combat the unfamiliar menace.

Mr Churchill, when Chancellor of the Exchequer a few years ago, in answer to a reasoned request for higher income-tax rebates for children, said that, while the aim of encouraging the professional classes to have more children was in every way praiseworthy, it had no connection with the Budget, whose only preoccupations were the finances of the country. It is precisely such a point of view which needs changing. In the long run, the quantity and quality of the country's population is its basic economic asset. Chancellors of the Exchequer already consider the effect of their proposals upon trade; there is every reason for them to consider their effect upon racial stability and racial health.

Finally, there remains the question of what I have styled long-range eugenics—the attempt to alter the character of the human race out of its present mould, to lead it on to new evolutionary achievements. We are sometimes told that the more likely fate for humanity is for it, like many another organic type, to pass its apogee and degenerate owing to the rise of other forms of life; and claimants for the biological throne have been named, such as the rat, or even, straying outside the vertebrate field, the ant or the termite. This prophecy we need not take too seriously. There is no likelihood of any other animal species becoming a biological rival to man. Man is unique among organisms in his power of speech and conceptual thought, which have resulted in his equally unique characteristics of an enduring and cumulative tradition and the power of making tools and machines. Thanks to these properties he has entrenched himself over a wider range of the globe's surface than any other kind of animal, and is in a position of dominance which would appear to be quite impregnable so long as he continues to cultivate his distinctively human characteristics, the proper exercise of which will inevitably make for further progress. Nowhere is the dictum, Unto him who hath shall be given, truer than in the spheres of competitive evolution : it is only when the progress of a given type is halted that others have the chance of ousting it.

Along these lines, the one possibility is that of self-caused degeneration of our species, leading to a collapse of the human domination which would then leave the door open for the rise of other forms of life. There are cases known in the paleontological history of life which can perhaps be best interpreted as a degeneration of the species due to some inherent decay of the germ-plasm, rather than to competition or changed conditions ; but we need not appeal to these ; for man is from the biological point of view very young, and no one acquainted with the evolutionary time-scale could possibly accuse him of racial senility. If the human race is to bring about its own collapse, it will be because it has counteracted the effects of natural selection without attempting to put anything in its place, has allowed harmful mutations to accumulate instead of weeding them out or prevented them from appearing, and in fine has neglected eugenic measures.

The commonest objection to such constructive eugenic ideas is that we do not know enough about the subject to decide upon the most desirable direction in which to push forward; that the views of, say, clerics, medical men, politicians, men of science, artists, business men and trades union leaders upon the most desirable type would be altogether at variance; and that in any case to entrust any body of men with the task of deciding who should be allowed to propagate, and who should not, would be to place too large and dangerous a power in their hands.

But this is to misrepresent the position. No eugenist in his senses ever has suggested, or ever would suggest, that one particular type or standard should be picked out as desirable, and all other types discouraged or prevented from having children. Here biology joins hands with common sense. The dictum of common sense, crystallized into a proverb, is that it takes all kinds to make a world. The evidence of biology, drawn from the facts of evolution, is that this dictum applies as much to different species and groups of animals and plants as to types within the one human species.

All ordinary people would agree that there are certain qualities which it is desirable for the race to possess. Among desirable qualities we should all put health and energy, physical and mental; special aptitudes, for music or mathematics, practical engineering or administrative genius, poetry or leadership; all-round qualities, such as general ability, perseverance, manual dexterity, humour, adaptability; and do not let us forget beauty. It is possible, and indeed probable, that certain desirable qualities in an individual exclude others: in any case, no one in his senses would set out to breed a race of supermen who should all combine the good qualities of, say, Keats, Henry Ford, Buddha, Abraham Lincoln, Adonis and Sir Isaac Newton. The task is a simpler one—to encourage the breeding of those with desirable qualities, even if they also possess defects in other qualities. It will be time enough after a thousand or ten thousand years of this to look into further questions, such as the precise proportion of poets, physicists and politicians required in a community, or the combination of a number of different desirable qualities in one human frame.

It is perfectly true that it is at the moment very difficult to envisage methods for putting even this limited constructive programme into effect. But this is due as much to difficulties inherent in our present social-economic organization as to our ignorance of human heredity, and most of all to the absence of a eugenic sense in the public at large.

A change in public opinion is indeed the first requisite. Dean Inge, in a recent essay, asserted that once a man has grasped the implications of biology in respect of evolution and inheritance, eugenics becomes for him not merely an important aim, but the most sacred ideal of the human race as a race. It becomes not merely an outlet for human altruism, but the outlet which is most comprehensive and of longest range of all outlets for altruism. It becomes, in fact, in Dean Inge's words, one of the supreme religious duties.

It is this attitude which we want to see grow and spread among civilized men and women, of every profession and of every class. Man has become what he is by a process of evolution which has taken perhaps a thousand million years; there is no reason why that evolution should not continue; and we can look forward, according to the astronomers, to at least another thousand million years of earth's habitability. If the past with its crude methods has taken life from single cells, or whatever simpler units it at first inhabited, to man, what may not man do in the future with the aid of conscious reason and deliberate planning?

Once that attitude has been assimilated, the idea of eugenics will take its proper place in our repertory of ideas. On its negative side, it becomes racial preventive medicine: on its positive side, racial hope.

And once this is so, the pressure of public opinion to get something done will become so great that something *will* be done. More minds will be set to amass the necessary knowledge, more will be detailed to think out ways and means of applying knowledge. We cannot yet see what those discoveries will be, or envisage the organization of a eugenic society. But knowledge will slowly grow, ways and means can surely be found. And so man may take up his birthright, which is to become the first organism exercising conscious control over its own evolutionary destiny.

CHAPTER IV

The Conflict between Science and Human Nature

THE rapid increase of scientific knowledge and the spread of the scientific spirit are in large part responsible for the strange and multiple chaos of the thought of Western countries to-day. This effect of science is often considered to be purely disintegrative. By sapping traditional systems, we are told, without putting anything adequate in their place, it has brought about this confusion. But, although this is in its measure true, it is far from being the whole truth. The chaos and confusion is largely due to the peculiar double-edged effect which scientific advance has had upon many of the pivots of our thought. Giving with one hand, she has taken away with the other. Pursuing abstract truth, she has often produced practical contradiction.

WHAT DARE I THINK?

One of the most obvious of the effects of science has been to confer upon man enormously enhanced power in dealing with the universe around him, and to hold out the prospect of a steady increase in this power. But, at the same moment, it has robbed him of his proud conviction of being the hero of the cosmic play, has deposed him from his seat in the centre of the universe, and relegated him to the position of an insignificant parasite produced by one of the satellites of one of millions of stars in one of millions of galaxies.

Advancing science has had an equally contradictory effect upon the religious outlook. By showing the baselessness of traditional theologies, it seemed at one time to be giving religion itself a mortal blow. But, when we come to look deeper, we find the unescapable fact of religious experience, which no scientific analysis can remove. Thus, by forcing religious thought to distinguish between theological scaffolding and religious core, science has actually encouraged the growth of a truer and more purely religious spirit. To put it in another way, if science has robbed religion of many of its certitudes, those certitudes were in a sphere improper to religion. True religious certitude is not in the realm of intellect at all, but concerns values and a special attitude towards them. Science has evicted religion from the universal but uneasy throne she occupied in the Middle Ages, but she has helped her to ascend her true and permanent throne of spiritual experience. After overthrowing supernaturalism, science is confronted with humanism.

Science, again, has made the human mind feel insecure by her insistence, in various fields, upon the notion of relativity. But if she has helped in the destruction of absolutist security, she has, through the idea of evolution, greatly stabilized thought by giving humanity a direction. And again, if biological studies have emphasized the incompleteness and in certain respects the unreality of any hard-and-fast conception of individuality, they have equally served as the charter of the individual as against the state or race or any organization of higher order, by insisting that the well-developed human individual, for all his limitations, is the highest product of evolution.

The multiple contradictions sum up along these lines—that in the sphere of control over environment and destiny, man is through science being given fabulous and undreamt-of powers, yet is by no means agreed as to how to employ them. And that in the sphere of thought, while the scientific picture of the universe, in which naturalism and determinism rule, grows ever more triumphant and complete, yet it becomes ever more sharply set off from the world of values in which the human spirit inevitably has its being. Science, in a word, both in the outer and the inner life, has come up against human nature, and each one seems in a strange confused way to be barring the progress of the other.

Science and human nature—there lies the chief unresolved antinomy of the present stage of our civilization. Every age has its own antinomies. That between Natural and

Supernatural is one, that between Human and Divine another; and there are the antinomies of mind and matter, individual and society, body and soul, magic and ordinary practice, and so on, each of which in its own time and place is or has divided thought. All such antinomies, however theoretical in their origin, can be of vital practical importance. To take but one, did not the Divine Right of Kings play an important political part? Was not the use of anaesthetics in childbirth reprehended as contrary to the will of God, and is not the same argument often used to-day against methods of birth-control and of eugenic sterilization?

But equally all such antinomies prove in the long run to be false or incomplete, the conflict between their two members by no means irreconcilable. In general, they arise from treating incomplete or slightly inaccurate premises as if they were final and accurate, and then pushing them to their logical conclusion; or from taking two partial views of reality, setting them up as complete and total, and then being surprised that they come into conflict.

It may be that reality is essentially unreasonable, truly disparate with itself, full of irreconcilable elements. Most of us, however, have a conviction that it is not; and even if, in ultimate analysis, this conviction seems to be more in the nature of faith than reasoned judgment, yet it must be said that the short history of human thought supports it. The increase of knowledge and of intellectual effort in analysis has repeatedly shown that conflicts can be avoided by a proper delimitation of function, and that apparent contradictions can be and are reconciled in a 'higher unity,' a broader synthesis.

When I spoke of the antinomy between science and human nature, I was using the word science loosely. I meant, of course, not that activity of human nature which produces scientific knowledge, but the fruits of it—the potentialities of control which it opens up, the picture of the universe which it provides. From our present point of view, the salient feature of the scientific picture of the universe is its neutrality in face of all the issues which to us as full human beings are so vital. Looked at objectively, the writ of our purely human values is seen to run over a negligible fraction of space and time : and of other values or purposes at work in the general operations of the universe, science can detect no trace, nor does she find any need to postulate them. Because these values are missing, there is a real and to many people alarming contrast between the cold scientific outlook and the immediacy and warmth of human knowledge and feeling, between the picture of the universe as an immense electronic dance-hall, in which an interminable succession of meaningless figures are executed, and the measuring-rod of human nature, with its scale of values, its demand for meaning in existence, its desires and aspirations and purposes.

But let us get to closer quarters with our problem ; and, first, with science and her place in our affairs. Science has two main functions in civilization. One is to give man

WHAT DARE I THINK?

a picture of the world of phenomena, the most accurate and complete picture possible. The other is to provide him with the means of controlling his environment and his destiny. Without the one, he can have no true orientation for his thought, no true conception of his place in the scheme of things, and so no proper programme for his aims. Without the other, he cannot maintain material progress, cannot achieve enduring organization, and so cannot compass the realization of whatever aims he may cherish.

But if he demands this help of science, then he must give her every possible assistance in all her legitimate fields and avocations, and must do his best to root out other systems of thought that are hostile to her. As an example, let us take magic—by which, of course, I do not solely mean professional witchcraft or organized mumbo-jumbo, but belief in mysterious powers and influences which are active for good or evil in the material world around us, and can be controlled, or at least propitiated, by methods wholly alien to those employed by science.

SCIENCE AND HUMAN NATURE

Magic in this sense is still to be found among a surprisingly large proportion of our human species—whether in the guise of the ordeals or divinations practised by African tribes, the processions to stop lava-flows or the prayers for rain still found in Christian countries, the refusals of civilized white men to light three cigarettes from one match or to sail on a Friday, or, among savages, the sacrifice of animals to promote the fertility of crops, or the eating of this or that flesh to ensure this or that quality in the eater.

Monsieur Allier has attempted to show in an interesting book, *The Mind of the Savage*, that it is the preponderance of belief in magic over belief in scientific naturalism which is the one great reason for the backward condition of so-called primitive peoples. Undoubtedly there is a great deal of truth in this contention. To it I would, however, add a second cause—the spreading over of religious emotion in a crude unselfcritical form into affairs where it has no business to meddle, with the consequent growth of irrational but powerful prohibitions and observances binding society in unreasoning conservatism.

The sense of sacredness is one of the main psychological springs of religion. But in origin the sacred is not necessarily all good. For one thing, as many anthropologists have pointed out, the animistic savage naturally finds 'bad-sacredness' as well as 'good-sacredness' in the welter of influences around him. For another, the element of fear which, albeit transmuted, new-combined, and sublimated, still enters into reverence or awe or any other emotion of man confronted with what he feels to be sacred, is inevitably more powerful in the dark uncomprehended world around the savage. Thus there grows up an irrational but potent fear of meddling, save by due magico-religious means, with anything to which sanctity adheres. And as the savage's uncritical religiosity comes to attach sanctity to a great many elements of his life, he speedily becomes entangled in a web of his own spinning, which, for all that it is invisible, is so charged with irrational emotion as

SCIENCE AND HUMAN NATURE

to keep him tightly imprisoned within its strands.

This has two morals to our present purpose. In the first place, we must combat the idea of magic wherever it lifts its head, in however up-to-date a guise it may appear. There is a real danger that the discoveries of science may become incomprehensible to the multitude. If so, they themselves may become invested with this very quality of magic that science, in making her discoveries, had to abjure. Witness the numerous quacks who trade on the supposedly mysterio-magical qualities of 'Electricity,' or the cranks who think they have evolved a complete theory of the universe by juggling with scientific terms like energy or magnetism, electron or relativity, which they have never properly grasped in their scientific bearing, but which they have proceeded to invest with quite unscientific qualities of essentially magic nature. Not only that, but if the discoveries of science are not understood, if they are regarded as so many incomprehensible but useful bags of tricks instead of various outcomes of the one fundamental and simple scientific method of work, the magic idea can play unchecked over other aspects of life. Only a few years back, it will be remembered, a Frenchwoman in Bordeaux succeeded in persuading a number of perfectly ordinary people among her bourgeois acquaintance that she was being bewitched by a certain priest, the Curé of Bourbon, and persuaded them so thoroughly that they assaulted him in his own sacristy, and beat him violently. Yet these people were living in one of the countries of the world in which science has had most to say.

The only way to dissipate this attitude of mind is by education. Every child must be taught something about science. And the science which is taught must not be a mere collection of facts and laws, imposed from without, unintelligibly, like a new Decalogue. With such treatment, the spirit of science escapes: and the spirit of science is as important to the proper understanding of the facts of science as it was to their original discovery. Much of the spirit of science is best brought home to the child's mind by some account of scientific history. The story of Galileo confounding authority by his famous but simple weight-dropping experiment, and all the consequences, in the shape of scientific mechanics, which flowed from it : how the early anatomists persisted in satisfying their thirst for knowledge, in spite of ecclesiastical prohibitions on dissection : the gradual way in which science arrives at her results, even without opposition from outside, as shown, for instance, in the growth of our ideas about such everyday affairs as combustion or respiration, or the more abstruse ideas of the atomic nature of matter or the conservation of energy : the Middle Ages' ignorance of the very idea of a gas, of the fact that the heart pumps the blood round the body, or that the child takes its origin from actual bits of living substance detached from the body of its parents—in these and a hundred other ways a realization can be built up of the slow invasion of science into fields where previously blank ignorance or misconception had been masters. If religious bodies should set themselves up to oppose such a treatment of science in schools, they will be mistaking their rightful sphere, and their opposition must at all costs be overcome.

In this historical treatment of scientific discovery, I see not merely one of the best ways of revealing the true essence of scientific method, but also a corrective to possible narrowness and dogmatism on the part of scientific specialists, a useful bridge between the scientific and the humanist sides of the school curriculum.)

But we can be and should be going on throughout life with the business of learning; and adult education is as important as school education.) In the United States a beginning has been made with a Science News Service for the popular Press. Such a service could play a great part; and if something similar were organized for the wireless, its usefulness would be still further extended. Men of science, in any case, cannot expect to have their results understood and appreciated unless they take some trouble to make them known and explain them to the uninitiated.

SCIENCE AND HUMAN NATURE

Our second moral is even more important. We must do our best to extend the use of scientific method into any and every field where it can be of use—that is to say, into every field in which we hope to exert reasoned control; and we must make this effort in spite of sanctities and susceptibilities. An obvious example is that of human population, its quantity and its quality. It is a matter of elementary arithmetic that population-increase cannot go on indefinitely. Of course, food-shortage and general discomfort will eventually bring about an equilibrium: but will not any such automatically arrived-at final state of population be overcrowded, poverty-stricken, and execrably uncomfortable compared with one kept deliberately at a lower but more orderly level?

It is equally a matter of simple arithmetic that, if different stocks multiply at different rates, the proportions of them which are in existence will alter, generation by generation. At present, for instance, Russians are multiplying much faster than Englishmen, while English miners are multiplying faster than English textile workers. There is also considerable evidence that, in civilized nations, the considerable body of people who are on the borderline between normal and definitely subnormal intelligence, are multiplying faster than the population as a whole. At the moment, confronted with such facts and fears, we do nothing. One of the chief reasons we do nothing is that love, marriage, the family, the act of reproduction—all of them intertwined with this business of population—are so emotionally charged, so impregnated with sanctities of one sort or another, that any attempt at scientific and therefore dispassionate study of the problems they raise is felt by many people as sacrilegious, any attempt to control them as unnatural.

In passing, the feeling which a very large number of people have about the act of reproduction itself affords a very good example of sacredness that is on the whole 'bad-sacredness.' When people attempt to convert it into 'good-sacredness,' as did William Blake (not to mention examples nearer home), they are usually branded as immoral. It is worth recalling that, in earlier times, similar religious objections were felt to the mere taking of a census—as when David felt he had 'sinned greatly' in numbering Israel (2 Sam. xxiv.). Different sanctities were here involved; and we to-day can see how baseless they were.

But our scientific humanism adopts as its guiding principle that we *can* consider everything in a scientific aspect, and that while doing so we must make every effort to rid ourselves of disturbing emotion. If we do succeed in discounting this powerful feeling about our reproductive functions—a feeling which, though unorganized, is identical in nature with much that we find organized in the religions of savages—the scales drop from our eyes and we see that, for instance, birth-control is no more 'unnatural' than wearing a top-hat, the regulation of human numbers and quality for the greater happiness and well-being of the race no more sacrilegious than the provision of proper water-supply or good education.

WHAT DARE I THINK?

The dangers of the opposition between science and humanism are many and obvious. The chief and central one is that scientific and humanist thought, failing to comprehend or sympathize with one another, shall organize themselves into two separate or even antagonistic streams, so that civilization shall be two-minded, in large part divided against itself, instead of single-minded, with a common main purpose and idea underlying all variety of minor difference. Every type of mind, if untempered by proper self-criticism, tends to retract into its own special narrowness. The vices of the scientific mind are intellectualism and lack of appreciation of the value of other kinds of experience, over-emphasis on doing and under-emphasis on being and feeling. The vices into which the humanistic mind tends to slip are contempt for the slow-but-sure methods of induction and experiment, acquiescent ignorance of the facts and laws of nature, belief in illusory short cuts to achievement.

A scientific humanism, in which science and human nature, natural law and spiritual

SCIENCE AND HUMAN NATURE

activity, are not opposed but united, is needed to unify the two opposing currents and resolve the antinomy. What do we mean by such an attitude of mind, and how can it be achieved? To attempt some answer to these questions will be my main purpose.

In the first place, it demands that we take a unitary view of the universe. The universe is not divisible into regions or compartments labelled natural and supernatural, material and spiritual, scientific and non-scientific, and so forth, as the surface of the globe is divisible into land and water. Either such labelling is a mere convenience for the mind, and gives names to two rather different parts of a single continuum; or it emphasizes different aspects of the single reality; or, finally, it is the result of investigating reality by different methods.

There are not two regions of reality, one of which is accessible to scientific method and the other inaccessible. Rather there is a single reality, but scientific and other ways of approaching it and treating it. Man's poems and religions, his values and hopes, are part of this single reality just as much as are the chemical elements or the geological strata. Do not let us forget that all we can be directly aware of is experience—an interacting of our mind with outer events); everything else is construction or abstraction) The very separation of experience into what is experienced and what experiences is an abstraction, and we reach further degrees of abstraction according to the way in which we sort and analyse our experience. (Science is the result of concentrating the mind's attack upon reality in one particular or restricted way; religion the result of concentrating it in a second and different way; art that of concentrating it in yet a third way; mathematics and philosophy in still other ways.

According to the restriction of attitude and approach, so will each activity have its particular restriction of usefulness. This is most obviously seen with mathematics. Very few people are concerned about a conflict between mathematics and religion, because mathematics has so obviously restricted its field that it fails to overlap appreciably

SCIENCE AND HUMAN NATURE

with the field picked out by the religious approach.

This has not been so clear with regard to science and religion. In the beginning this was due to a failure of the religious approach to realize its restrictions, with the result that it trespassed and poached, annexed fields not its own, and then, feeling that possession was nine points of the law, strenuously objected to relinquishing them when the true claimant appeared. Of late years, science has often shown a similar failure to recognize her own limitations. She has attempted to treat religious experience as a meaningless or even a pathological phenomenon, or has asserted that the scientific attitude can simply be substituted for the religious. But, recently, there has been a determined attempt at delimitation of scientific and religious function by men such as Broad and Whitehead and Eddington. The possibility of orderly co-operation between science and religion now exists, although it is too much to expect of human nature to hope that spiritual Chauvinism, whether religious or scientific, will not long continue to overstep the prescribed boundaries and to provoke opponents.

Religion is concerned with a complex emotional attitude of the human personality towards the universe as it impinges upon him. There is always the attempt to grasp this impinging reality as a single whole and to react to it with a movement of the whole inner being; although the imperfections of knowledge and of thought almost always keep these unities from being fully realized. The religious attitude of inner towards outer involves a specific emotional attitude, into which the feeling of sacredness or holiness always enters, even if sometimes in debased or rudimentary form; and it involves value. Science, on the other hand, deliberately rejects emotion and values both from her attitude and her method. Her sole aim is intellectual, her sole method statistical, comparative, or metrical. She can discuss values, but only objectively; she can herself experience none, save the value of truth. No emotion and no sanctity must stand in the way of her investigations; and she cannot be successful unless she is dispassionate. She exhibits the curious and instructive paradox that only by suspending judgment does she arrive at truer judgment, only by banishing the driving force of emotion and the false certitude of the will-to-believe from her methods does she arrive at greater power and greater certitude.

Religion must recognize that theology is not religion but science—and, in all its orthodox forms, extremely poor science at that. And science must recognize that, while for some aspects of the business of living, the scientific approach is best, for others the religious approach is more important. Needham in his recent book, *The Sceptical Biologist*, epigrammatically sums up the position by pointing out that we have just as much right and just as much reason to ask whether the spiritual life is any obstacle to materialism, as the more usual question whether materialism is any obstacle to the spiritual life.

The scientific and the religious approaches to experience are different functions of the human spirit. The dangerous opposition between them comes when over-specialization produces a whole class of individuals with scientific hypertrophy and religious atrophy, another class with scientific atrophy and religious hypertrophy. This is an attempt to follow the methods of the bees and ants; in their unintelligent societies, in which tradition and education play no part, it is the only method available. But human society is built up on quite other lines. Man is the only social organism whose individuals can be both specialized and generalized at once, and can develop hypertrophically in regard to one faculty without corresponding atrophy of others. And since mutual understandings and a common tradition constitute the basis of human progress, it is therefore extremely important that any machine-like or ant-like specialization should be avoided, for this inevitably prevents mutual understanding and destroys the unity of the social tradition. Science, as a body of knowledge and principle, is essentially a means. She is a direction-post; and she provides the only way of achieving distant and elaborate ends. But, as we all know well, she can be used to compass any ends, of destruction as of construction, of selfish gain as of communal benefit.

It is human nature which dictates ends for which science must provide the means. Science, as I say, can provide human nature with maps and direction-posts, by helping man to understand himself and by showing more clearly his relation to his environment. In the last fifty or sixty years, for instance, evolutionary science has provided new ends, new outlets for human nature, by demonstrating the universal pliability of organisms under selection, by opening up astounding vistas of future time before our race, and so by holding out the vision of human progress from our present chaotic state, as a goal for action.

But its action is only demonstrative. It can show us goals, but not impel us towards them. The springs of action lie elsewhere. When we come to action we are in a realm wholly different from that of science. For action is always entangled with motive, motive is always part feeling. The activity of human nature has its being in and through that scale of values which science by her very method banishes from herself.

In so far as science is human activity and not the outcome of that activity, it too, of course, owes its existence to motive and is bound up with value. Human nature is curious, it wants to know things and to get at the truth, it values knowledge both for the pure pleasure of knowing and for the power which it brings. If this were not so, our laboratories would not be full of scientific workers; for the material recompenses of a scientific career are not comparable with those open to the professional or the business man. But we are talking of science as the body of knowledge and the power of control gained by scientific activity; and these, we repeat, are in themselves neutral, uncharged with emotion, untroubled by ideas of value.

Then, while science is a body of rules and laws, humanism is an affair not of rules (or rather, not merely of rules) but of uniques—unique things, unique events. And these uniques have each their value. Every work of art, for instance, whether poem or picture, a building or a piece of music, is first and foremost *itself*, or it is nothing. It says something on its own account; what it says may be something general, but it says it in its own new and individual way. If it does not do this, it ceases to be a real work of art, and, artistically speaking, tells you nothing you want to know. It obviously has to obey certain rules (as a poem to scan, a building to stand up, and so on), but it is much more than its rules.

Human beings are all up to a point alike, but they are also all unique, both in their constitution and in the circumstances of their lives. (History repeats itself; but never exactly.)

Scientific laws on the other hand are essentially statistical laws: they deal with the resultants of the action of huge numbers of separate objects, or with the averages of enormous sequences of events.

Humanism in its various aspects is always concerned with the value of the particular. The rules of painting have no aesthetic value, but each picture has its own unique value. A wife is not just any woman, a friend not just any man. (A moral act is a particular resultant in particular circumstances) (the value which knowledge has in and for itself is the value of individual illumination)

The only way in which the conflict between science and human nature can be ended is by combining science and the other fruits of the human spirit in a new alliance, a new attitude, to which we may give the name of Scientific Humanism. But to deal with the implications of this new alignment will need a fresh chapter.

CHAPTER V

Scientific Humanism

THE conflict between science and human nature can only be reconciled in an attitude and a temper of mind which may fittingly be called scientific humanism. In the present chapter I shall try to set out some of the implications of this attitude.

To begin with, we must enquire a little more deeply into what we mean by humanism, what we think to be its aims, what its scale of values. One sentence, to my mind, really contains them all—to have life, and to have it more abundantly. Although, like all one-sentence programmes, this needs amplification and definition, it proclaims at the outset the humanist's main creed: that the sole source of values which we know of in the universe is the commerce between mind and matter that we call human life;

for it generates not only our standard of values, but the experiences, objects and ideas which are of highest concrete value in themselves :) (that life as a whole is more important than any single part or product of life :¡ and that, since life, however complex, is essentially one, it is false to give absolute predominance to any system of ideas or conduct, or indeed to any one aspect of life.

A Humanism that is also scientific sees man endowed with infinite powers of control should he care to exercise them. More importantly, in the perspective of scientific knowledge, it sees man against his true background—a background of the irresponsible matter and energy of which he is himself composed, of the long and blind evolution of which he is himself a product. Humanity thus appears as a very peculiar phenomenon —a fraction of the universal world-stuff which, as result of long processes of change and strife, has been made conscious of itself and of its relations with the rest of the world-stuff, capable of desiring, feeling, judging and planning.) It is an experiment of the universe in rational self-consciousness. (So far as we are yet aware, it is the only such experiment; but that is a matter of minor importance.) Any value which it has, apart from its selfish value to itself, resides in this fact.

The apprehension of values depends upon a balancing of motives and ideas; a standard of values demands conceptual thought. Even the highest animals have only the barest rudiment of such possibilities. But once man, by the aid of language, could think abstract thoughts, a new framework was generated, a framework as important to mental life as the skeletal framework to bodily life—the framework of universals and ideals. This is an immediate by-product of language and logic. It is impossible to pronounce the simplest judgment—'this is true' or 'that is not true'—without implicitly setting up a category of abstract truth. Once you can argue whether an action is right or wrong, you presuppose an ideal of rightness. You may not consciously envisage such ideals, but your own or others' logic will sooner or later lead you to them. The humanist sees no other absolute quality in truth or goodness than this. It is a similar absoluteness that inheres in mathematical reasoning. Once you have the power of inventing numbers and abstracting the idea of number from other qualities, you can go on to the mathematics of imaginary quantities or fictitious dimensions.

The actual way in which these abstract ideas are applied as standards of value is subject to change. The ideas about truth held by a believer in verbal inspiration must be different from those of one trained in the methods of philosophy or of mathematical physics. Just as the bodily skeleton was moulded and improved during the course of its evolution, so this spiritual framework grows and is modified during human history.

The different emphasis laid upon this world and the next, for instance, has produced very different measuring-rods for Goodness in the minds of the mediæval theologian and the modern social worker. Again, many religious minds have found

SCIENTIFIC HUMANISM

acceptance of a fixed creed the highest good, because they believe it the only avenue to salvation. To the evolutionist, who knows the variety but incompleteness of life, and the necessity for change, this good turns to bad.

These universals are but frameworks. To revert to our metaphor, they resemble the archetypal plans of construction of this or that animal organ which have no concrete existence (save in the pages of zoological text-books), but yet underlie and in part determine the construction of every actual organ. The archetypal plan of vertebrate skeleton could be pinched and pulled to support a flying or a swimming or a running creature. The framework of our abstract and universal ideas can be practically moulded in a not dissimilar adaptive way.

In the course of its evolution, human life comes to generate new experiences, new ways of living and of expression, which are concretely of value in themselves; in this way new qualities and also new heights of value are attained. Stoicism was the means of giving the world a new type of character. Dante's *Vita Nuova* was the expression of a new way of love between man and woman which in previous ages had not been possible. The transference of the sense of supreme sacredness from fear to love, accomplished by Jesus, led man to wholly new levels of religious value. (Pure knowledge has absolute value : and in the intellectual comprehension of the world about us given by Newton, by Darwin, or by the latest discoveries in astrophysics, science has produced something new and valuable.) Beethoven, in his posthumous quartets and other late works, produced something wholly new in the world. It is not new knowledge of the external world, as Mr Sullivan in his *Beethoven* would wish us to believe, but knowledge of new capabilities of the human spirit—new experience.

In all such cases, of course, others may not be capable of appreciating the new-found value, may not wish to employ it. But the value has been created ; it is there, waiting to be used.

One of the functions of humanity in its

SCIENTIFIC HUMANISM

evolutionary experiment is thus, it seems, the creating of new experiences of value, in any and every realm, from character to pure intellect, from religion to art.

As a matter of history, the course of events in this progressive change of framework and progressive realization of new value has so far been rather a curious one. At the risk of over-simplification, I may put it thus. In primitive man, and in many of the uneducated to-day, different values are not much thought about or analysed, but just accepted. Each separate activity as it happens to come along is instinctively valued for its immediate satisfaction. Further, since the value of many later and more complex human experiences cannot be felt by a mind which is not trained or not set in a certain direction (I do not suppose you could ever get a Masai warrior to see that there was ' anything in ' the *Vita Nuova*; any more than a wholly untrained mind could be thrilled by reading the latest cosmogony by Jeans or Eddington), the experiences regarded as valuable are themselves more primitive.

WHAT DARE I THINK?

A large part of early man's values must have been concerned with physiological satisfaction, his life a series of activities only very partially related in thought, his various mental activities existing in more or less 'thought-tight' compartments. But just because he was not too logical, and because he was endowed with a variety of instinctive impulses, his life, though on a low level, was full and varied.

Man's intellectual faculties, hovering protectively over his naked feelings and desires, have doubtless always done something to cloak them with the respectability of Reason —or, at least, of reasons. But in the beginnings of society this rationalizing power must have been very incomplete and un-co-ordinated. With settled civilization, the reflective mind had new leisure and new opportunities. The result was apparent in the various theological and philosophical schemes aiming at some degree of logic and completeness, which have characterized the last three or four thousand years.

It was as if the human spirit, growing more

fully conscious of itself, its needs and its defects, its strange isolation in an incomprehensible and often hostile world, felt the imperative need of some support, some framework of authority outside the individual and, if possible, outside the species, some relief from vague fears and speculations by means of clear-cut explanations.

In passing, it is not only in the matter of abstract frameworks or rationalizing explanations that this demand for external sanctions showed itself. For instance, as Pierre Janet has pointed out, the insistence on oaths which characterized the mediæval period was an attempt to buttress up the sense of truth and honesty, which ought to have an inner sacredness of its own, with purely external sanctities. The excessive use of vows, in the same way, is an attempt to screw external sanctions on to our own infirm purpose ; it is interesting to find that this falling back upon vows, combined with over-scrupulosity, is a frequent symptom of certain kinds of neurotic disease.

The support may have been needful ; but

it was in danger of becoming a prison. Abstract thought can be so devastating just because it is general, because of its apparent absoluteness. There is no gainsaying logic. Once you cease to have the saving grace of humility, and believe that you possess any final or definitive knowledge of the nature of things, whether off your own bat or conferred by external grace of revelation, you are doomed if you make the appeal to logic. Your premises are bound to be incomplete; and the inaccuracy, multiplied by the chain of levers which logic provides from particular to general, at the last assumes portentous proportions.

If you really believed the mediæval Christian schemes you were bound to be intolerant, bound to persecute and establish inquisitions. If you really believe in the divine ordinance of kingship or marriage, or that the Decalogue was divinely ordained, you cannot help drawing certain practical conclusions which will in time put you in violent opposition to the humanist view on such subjects.

SCIENTIFIC HUMANISM

That period of human evolution which we may call the period of the great theological religions, was from this point of view one in which perplexed human beings, in their struggle with the outer world, with other human beings, and most of all with the tortuous inconsistencies and treacheries of the human spirit, found much-needed help in the fixity of generalized schemes of thought. They discovered that they could gain support from abstract ideas such as those of reason or justice; from unattainable but absolute ideals, as of goodness or truth, from the unassailable logic of complete schemes of creation and salvation. The externalizing of the compulsive but changeable inner voice of impulse and conscience in outer authority and codes of divine revelation was another method of finding support, and the psychological trickery involved in this projection of inner feeling into outer sanction was so simple and natural to untutored thinking that it passed unnoticed.

But the method had its inevitable defects. Grateful support could become imperceptibly converted into cramping rigidity. The inevitable slight pre-eminence given to this or that quality in the original scheme of thought could become magnified by logic into an entire one-sidedness. The general and abstract could be taken for the absolute and complete, and so the way barred to novelty or fresh achievements.

In the last half-millennium there has been a change. Thought has not only attacked the rigidity of the old schemes, but has also devoted itself to new creation. The absoluteness and externality of the old frameworks are gone. Scientific law, for instance, is no longer regarded as the transcription of some prodigious code laid up in heaven, but as the most convenient way in which our human intellect can sum up the controllable aspects of phenomena.

The new attack has at last invaded the citadel itself. No longer can we set matter against life; or life against mind; or mind as against spirit, as two essentially different realms.

The time is beginning to ripen in which we

SCIENTIFIC HUMANISM

can attempt to recover a greater elasticity of our framework by going back to the beginning, to the nature of things and the nature of man as seen in the light of new knowledge, and building up our scheme anew. This new humanism, if we attempt it, must, in the first place, attempt to do justice to the variety of human nature and refrain from giving pre-eminence to any one aspect—a task which demands a difficult combination of altruism and tolerance. It must attempt to do justice to our incompleteness, and the constant change in knowledge and outlook which we must hope for. This demands a sacrifice almost intolerable to certain minds—the sacrifice of certitude. It must finally attempt to provide some real and strong framework of support, and so prevent the exaggerated individualism, the social disintegration and the tolerance that turns to indifferentism, which have characterized other humanistic periods such as the early Roman Empire or the Renaissance.

Humanism, with the aid of the picture given by Science, *can* achieve a framework strong enough for support. In the light of evolution, she can see an unlimited possibility of human betterment. And she can see that possibility as a continuation of the long process of biological betterment that went before the appearance of man. If humanism cannot have the fixed certitude of dogma, it can at least have a certitude of direction and aim. The altruistic forces of human nature need not be restricted to isolated acts of doing good. They can harness themselves for the task, inspiring because of its very size, of slowly moving mankind along the upward evolutionary path.

The other certitude it can lay claim to is the certitude of its own values. They cannot be disputed—they are simply experienced. Any one who has experienced the illumination of new knowledge, or the ecstasy of poetry or music, or the deliberate subordination of self to something greater, or the self-abandonment of falling in love, or complete physical well-being, or the intense satisfaction of a difficult task achieved, or has had a mystical experience, knows that they are in

SCIENTIFIC HUMANISM

some way valuable for their own sakes beyond ordinary every-day satisfactions, such as being more or less fit, earning one's own living, or filling one's belly. We must see to it that our pursuit of these experiences does not conflict with other sides of our nature, or with other human beings; here, again, what is absolute in its own right is purely relative within the general scheme. But the values are there and are real, and there is some general consensus as to their scale of grading. The difficulty for many minds is that these values are of our own generating, not in any way endowed with external authority. But in the religious sphere, was it not Jesus who laid down once and for all that the kingdom of heaven is within us? As if we abandon the idea of external certitude for scientific law, we need not worry about doing so for our scheme of values.

At the present moment we have no policy of values such as, at least in theory, the Middle Ages possessed. The world is but limited in size; yet we permit this or that incomplete idea to go spreading patchily over its surface almost without reference to what else it may make impossible. If there is one thing which is obvious it surely is that economic aims are not a final end in themselves. To be prosperous is a prerequisite to innumerable other activities; but prosperity is not the chief measure by which we should judge success. The same applies to the quantitative mania for which American cities have been famous, but from which no nation is really exempt—the mania which assumes that what matters is the number of people in a town irrespective of their qualities or what they are doing, the amount of money spent on a building irrespective of its beauty, and so on.

Quite recently an opponent of one of the bills for preventing the destruction of rural amenities wrote pointing out that this would cause certain financial losses; as the bill concerned itself 'after all with merely aesthetic considerations,' these could not be justified!

Without any general scheme of values, we take a whole series of human needs and aims in turn, pretend that each is somehow absolute, try to push it to its logical conclusion, and then let them fight it out. In the resultant chaos, of course, many other subtler values languish or are left on one side. The value of human life becomes so absolute that it is murder to put away a deformed monster at birth, and criminal to suggest euthanasia; and we push on with our reduction of infant mortality until we save an excess of cripples and defectives to breed from.

The enhanced control that is in our hands, and the fact that much of the world is actually filling up, are at last giving us pause. The Indian mortality rate could doubtless be reduced by half—but what would you do with the increased population? Even if you bring huge areas of arid Indian land under irrigation and cultivation, it is only a matter of a generation or so before the new vacant space will be overrun by new population on the same low level of prosperity, health and education as the old. Have you done any good by causing more babies to live and so creating greater population-pressure, or by opening up new land to be filled at once by the human flood? Might it not have been better to have left the death side of nature's population-control to itself until we had some future policy for dealing simultaneously with birth, or to have kept some open spaces in reserve until there was some better reason for filling them? At the moment most people do not even put such questions, (much less try to answer them)

In England itself, the tiny size of the country has at last forced us to ask ourselves questions of this kind. Here, again, we have let each partial aim be carried out without reference to a general policy and are suddenly awakening to the fact that they are all cutting each other's throats. At last we have begun to ask what we want to live for, and to realize that the intangible values must be planned and worked for as much as the tangible ones, that there are people to whom solitude and wild nature provide some of the highest values in their lives, as there are others to whom social intercourse is the greatest pleasure.

SCIENTIFIC HUMANISM

Humanism thus would try to plan its limited physical environment so that within it different values are balanced and do not conflict too disastrously. This is a fairly obvious step to take. But a subtler reaction of the humanist point of view will be its influence upon our equally limited individual lives. With the decay of rigid codes, rigid schemes of valuation, rigid ideas of externally imposed law, we need be much less the victims of consistency.

There is value in logical thought; so there is in mystical experience. Because, for the moment, we cannot intellectually grasp why the mystical experience is of value, we need not reject it, any more than we need reject the value of logical thought because it does not give the peace or sense of completion produced by the mystical experience.

Self-sacrifice and asceticism can be experienced as of the utmost value; so can self-expression or the fullest satisfaction of bodily needs. It is very difficult, however, for some people to think that they or any one else can be genuine in deliberately practising what are loosely called self-denial and self-indulgence at different times. So long, however, as the impulse to either is genuine, both can be of value, and it is often only the demon of consistency which prevents us from achieving the needed genuineness of impulse. Both purge the soul and nourish it, though in different ways, and we have to accept that as fact, instead of trying to explain it away by logic. Even should we eventually choose one way or one activity as having supreme value for us, we must not deny the right of others to choose differently. And, also, we are not likely to practise our choice well unless we have had experience of other activities. It is no coincidence that many saints, like Augustine or Francis, began by enjoying the variety of life's ordinary joys to the full.

Do not let it be supposed that I am preaching hedonism, even a spiritualized hedonism. Hedonism, like utilitarianism, is another of these paper schemes, beautifully logical, that just are not true. The humanists, looking into human nature, must acknowledge that effort is often its own reward, that pain may

SCIENTIFIC HUMANISM

be essential to development, that limitation is frequently a prerequisite to achievement. He finds the desire for a sacrifice and self-mortification just as natural and almost as widespread as the desire for achievement and self-assertion—and sees that the one tendency is just as dangerous and unpleasant as the other if indulged in the wrong way. And he sees, looking beyond man by the light of science, that all these qualities have their counterpart in biological evolution, and all seem necessary for the advancement of the evolutionary experiment. Sacrifice and self-assertion are both biological necessities in their place and time; without effort there could be no survival, without pain no surmounting of harm, without limitation of possibility no realization of actual biological success.

The difference between human and biological affairs is that man, through his new powers of mind, has reached a new stage. From the purely biological standpoint, the main criteria are survival and reproduction. Man has entered a realm where things and experiences can have a supreme value in themselves without subserving any purely biological needs. The love immortalized in the *Vita Nuova* has been spiritualized away from its original connection with reproduction. A life devoted to pure music or pure mathematics has no counterpart whatever among lower organisms. Up till now most of the energies of the human race have been devoted to the biological needs of individual and racial survival. But now we are at least able to envisage a future in which the control of environment provided by science will be so effective that only a small fraction of human energy need be devoted to merely biological ends. The rest will be free to satisfy itself as it wishes. One of the problems of the past has been to keep the sense of values unimpaired by disease, misery and grinding poverty. A serious problem of the future will be how to keep values unimpaired by superabundance of leisure.

At the moment there are vast possibilities of value running to waste because they are not harnessed, or because they are not even realized. The number of subtle and individual minds that find themselves unable to join wholeheartedly in any corporate organization is increasing; they find themselves over-individualized, incapable of experiencing many of the values which come from losing self. The organizations in which the individual can lose himself and taste self-sacrifice and corporate enhancement, are for the most part blatantly irrational, like political parties, or committed to out-of-date or one-sided ideas like most of the churches; or, like public schools, they encourage crude and juvenile loyalties; or, as in the teamwork of sport, satisfy only a limited part of human nature.

One real task for humanism as I see it is to develop organizations which shall satisfy the need for corporate action and loyalty, the desire we all have to feel of use, and shall satisfy the urge to self-sacrifice as well as intellectual aspirations. The New Samurai of Wells' *A Modern Utopia* embodied a similar idea. The success they might have is foreshadowed by the success already attending such imperfect adumbrations of the idea as the Boy Scouts or the various 'Youth Movements' in Central Europe. I do not think it would be impossible to build up a scheme of the sort in connection with education, though at present every one not already committed to organizations is too much ashamed of showing enthusiasm in unfashionable ways to begin planning along the proper lines and on the proper scale.

The fact is that no community has ever yet set itself seriously to the task of scientific humanism. No nation has really attempted to think out what are the valuable things in life and the relation between them, or to work out the best means of realizing these values in fullest intensity and proper relative dosage. A few individual thinkers have tried their hands, but until society as a whole gets busy with the problem, individual attempts will have little effect.

Is it possible to plan a body which shall engender enthusiasm and canalize devotion after the fashion of a young religious order, but which shall not fall into the dangers of religious dogmatism on the one hand, and on

SCIENTIFIC HUMANISM

the other shall not by defects in its organization slip into the conservatism or worldliness which is the usual fate of so many orders?

Is it possible to organize a body of opinion which shall combine the enthusiasm of a political party with the suspension of judgment of the scientific investigator? Is it possible during education to give the average boy and girl such a taste for various values—beauty in art, say, or beauty in nature—that they will cherish them throughout life? At present we stuff them with facts so as quite to ruin their taste for knowledge, and leave other values to look after themselves.

It is the custom to say that modern psychology delights in revealing the most unsavoury motives to our most respectable actions. It was Freud himself, however, who said that if the average man was in some ways much more immoral than he suspected, he is in others much more moral. There is, in fact, a reserve of the angelic in ordinary people, which is unused and even unsuspected, because it does not fit with everyday ideas, because, in fact, we, most of us, are subconsciously rather apologetic about such impractical and inconvenient idealisms. Is there a way of tapping this reserve of moral power without letting it loose in the form of irrational prejudice or wild fanaticism, moral, religious or patriotic? On these and hundreds of similar questions we are blankly ignorant. We build laboratories to test out how we can harness and concentrate electrical and chemical and mechanical forces; but the corresponding problem of harnessing and intensifying the latent powers and activities of human nature we have scarcely even begun to envisage.

I must bring this rambling chapter to its end. Scientific humanism is a protest against supernaturalism: the human spirit, now in its individual, now in its corporate aspects, is the source of all values and the highest reality we know. It is a protest against one-sidedness and fixity: the human spirit has many sides and cannot be ruled by any single rule; nor can it be restrained from making new discoveries in the adventure of its evolution. It insists that the same scientific procedure can

SCIENTIFIC HUMANISM

be applied to human life as has been applied with such success to lifeless matter and to animals and plants—scientific survey, study and analysis, followed by increasing practical control. It insists on human values as the norms for our aims, but insists equally that they cannot adjust themselves in right perspective and emphasis except as part of the picture of the world provided by science. It realizes that human desires and aspirations are the motive power of life, but insists that no long-range or comprehensive aim of humanity can ever be realized except with the aid of the pedestrian and dispassionate methods, the systematic planning, the experimental testing which can be provided only by science.

At the moment, a particular task of scientific humanism is to clarify her own ideas as to the limitations of the various activities of the human mind. To take but three: Science is a way of collecting and handling experience of the controllable aspects of phenomena. Religion is a way of experiencing the impact of the outer universe on the personality as a whole : <u>the universe and human personality being what they are, this way of experience will always involve some feeling of sacredness.</u> Art is a way of expressing some felt experience in communicable form ; and a way which always involves that most difficult of things to define, the aesthetic emotion. Each selects and correlates in its own special way out of the common flux of experience. Each tells you something about reality—science more about the external aspects of it which can be controlled either in thought or practice ; religion more about the kingdom of heaven that is within us ; art about the fusion of inner and outer in individual experiences of value in themselves. Each is limited in its scope and its bearings, but can be universally applied.

In my phrase, scientific humanism, I have chosen to emphasize science as against all the other human activities for a simple reason—that at the moment science is in danger of setting itself up as an external code or framework as did revealed religion in the past ;

and only by putting it in its rightful place in the humanist scheme shall we avoid this dangerous dualism. But if science must beware of trying to become a dictator, the other human activities must beware of the jealousy which would try to banish the upstart from their affairs. The only significance we can see attaching to man's place in nature is that he is willy-nilly engaged in a gigantic evolutionary experiment by which life may attain to new levels of achievement and experience. Without the impersonal guidance and the efficient control provided by science, civilization will either stagnate or collapse, and human nature cannot make progress towards realizing its possible evolutionary destiny.

CHAPTER VI

Science, Religion and Human Nature

IT remains, finally, to discuss some of the bearings of scientific discovery upon that deepest-twined and most complex part of man's intangible environment of thought and feelings—his religion. When I delivered the lecture upon which these two chapters are based, I received what I thought was rather more than my due share of public attack. It was, however, somewhat of a comfort that I was attacked from both sides—attacked just as bitterly and vigorously by the out-and-out rationalists and free-thinkers as by representatives of the churches. To be sure, the fact of being attacked from both sides is no proof of excellence; but it is at least some guarantee that I was not being so extreme as some of my orthodox opponents appeared to imagine. And with this preface I will embark directly upon my subject.

* * * * * *

I had occasion not long ago to look up some of the late nineteenth-century controversies between science and religion, controversies in which the protagonists were men like Gladstone and my grandfather; controversies which shook the world of thought of the time. And I must confess that I found them by no means dull, but dead. It was astonishing how lifeless those disputes seemed after only half a century.

For the argument was largely about matters which seem rather unimportant to-day—whether the Mosaic account of creation was literally or even symbolically accurate, whether Jonah was really swallowed by a whale, whether there was a historical Flood or no. The dispute was really between scientific common-sense and freedom of thought on the one hand and religious authoritarianism and the theory of verbal inspiration on the other. These controversies killed the pretensions of orthodoxy as dead as mutton;

and it is no longer possible for the fight to take place on the same ground, the argument to start from the same premisses. Sometimes, it is true, incidents like the Dayton evolution trial or the Prayer-book controversy remind us of the strength of antiquated ideas or non-rational feelings in religious matters; but it is no longer possible for the world of thought to take such matters seriously (save as sociological phenomena); the spokesmen of religion no longer choose such ground on which to give battle; and the living interest of the discussion has moved to another sphere.

It is interesting to speculate as to the attitude which the great nineteenth-century champions of freedom of thought and religious liberalism would have taken up on the question if they were alive and in the fullness of their powers to-day. In an essay written for the centenary of my grandfather's birth, on his attitude towards religion, I wrote the following passage: 'He was forced by the intransigent attitude of Victorian orthodoxy first of all to think of God in orthodox terms

—cruder terms, in all probability, than he would have arrived at if he had been free to excogitate the problem for himself in quiet and on its merits ; and, secondly, to adopt an agnosticism which was not passive, no merely fainéant intellectual gesture, but implied the positive immorality of attempts to draw conclusions from premisses which could not be known—the immorality, therefore, of basing a religion on the attributes of the type of God with which his opponents, or certainly the majority of them, confronted him.'

Moncure Conway I did not know personally. But from the testimony of his writings and of those who knew him it seems that he was of somewhat different temperament from Thomas Huxley, his colleague in the work of liberating the religious spirit. He could not escape the intellectual climate of his age, nor the theological difficulties which the dead hand of orthodoxy forced on all those of the age who endeavoured to think for themselves. But his main preoccupations were less intellectual than ethical and practical. Above all, he combined a devotion to religion with a rare and embracing humanism. It is for that reason above all others that I was proud to have been chosen as one of the lecturers in the foundation associated with his name, for to my mind an enlightened humanism such as his is the greatest need of the world to-day.

To recall such men is inspiring. But it is also melancholy, for they are gone and we have need of them. Would that such vital souls and piercing intellects were here with us to help in taking the dispute between science and religion a stage further towards adjustment! For I confess that I see several dangers in the present situation. One is the premature attempt to cut the Gordian knot by means of philosophic mysticism, as exemplified by Bergson and Driesch, and in more recent times in rather a different form by Whitehead and Eddington. It is not unfair, I think, to say that the net result of the thesis maintained by such writers is something like this: the scientific account of things ends in obscurity and irrationality; let us accordingly introduce a corresponding dose of unintelligibility on the philosophic and religious side, and then the accounts will balance.

Another very different danger comes from the complacently destructive attitude of many representatives of rationalist thought. They, it seems, have not realized that the real battle has moved elsewhere, and continue to fight with the camp-followers of the other side as if these were the main army. Half a century ago destruction was the prime necessity: the false claims of authority and inspirationism had to be broken down before the free spirit of religion could emerge. But now, though much minor destruction is still necessary, the prime need is construction. Construction, indeed, is busily at work, but much of it is ill-informed and misguided. Some liberals are so busy flogging the dead horses of last generation's orthodoxy that they seem unaware of this generation's multifarious upthrustings of the religious spirit. When I was younger a widely-posted advertisement assured the world that 'Mazawattee Tea reminds you of the delicious blends of thirty years ago.' We do not want any of this *Mazawatteeism* in the domain of liberal religious thought.

The forms which these new manifestations may assume are varied and sometimes extraordinary. We have the exasperating pseudo-mysticism of the 'New Thought' organizations; the portentous success of Spiritualism; the continued expansion of Christian Science; the growth of Anglo-Catholicism within the Church of England, indicating a tendency to think less of dogma and to extract all that is possible out of the ritual and actions of worship and the communal religious experience; the increased tolerance over doctrinal matters which has fostered the strong movement towards union or re-union among the various Protestant Churches. Some of these manifestations may appear only as new growths of old ecclesiasticism, others as lamentable examples of human silliness or credulity; but all testify to the vitality of the religious spirit seeking expression, and to the vast amount of constructive work to be done by those who

SCIENCE, RELIGION AND HUMAN NATURE

possess the religious spirit, but are also capable of free and liberal thinking.

In both these cases the difficulties of which I have spoken have arisen as the result of a reaction against an already existing wrong attitude. The mysticism of some modern philosophers is due to a reaction against the aridity of a world without values, against the complacent over-simplifications of certain exponents of science or of materialistic philosophy. The unconstructive attitude of some of the left wing among religious thinkers is due to their reaction against old-fashioned orthodoxy's pernicious habit of accepting myth as fact, symbol as infallible truth, ritual acts as possessed of magic power.

This latter reaction, inevitable and salutary in its time, has had another influence upon many of the bodies standing for the free advance of religious thought, which will need to be corrected before they can bring their full weight to bear in construction. They have had to suffer so much from myth masquerading as fact that they have hardly attempted to see whether myth, stripped of its disguise, may not still have a valuable rôle to play in religion; they have become so sick of loose symbolic thinking that they have attempted to do without symbols; they see so clearly the degrading effect on intellect and character of belief in the magical efficacy of ritual words or acts that they have been afraid of ritual. As a result, they frequently tend to become jejune, cold, and dry, and do not appeal to the common man, full-bodied and comparatively unreflective as he is. Thus, though there are exceptions, the more intellectual among the liberal movements in religion have tended to grow thin, the less intellectual to be merely woolly.

The remedy is for all who are interested in the development of religion to make a new start. If others adopt points of view that to us seem old-fashioned, silly, or wrong, do not let us pay them the compliment of reacting against them; to do this means that we recognize common premisses, a common basis of thought, with them. Do not let us concern ourselves with outworn disputes; error dies hard, but, once new truth shows,

SCIENCE, RELIGION AND HUMAN NATURE

it is more profitable to follow the truth and build according to its lights than to engage in the slow and less valuable task of accelerating error's disagreeable death-throes. The nineteenth century has shown, or so many of us believe, that a whole spawn of monstrous ideas about religion—verbal inspiration, eternal damnation, magical efficacy of prayer or formula or rite, miraculous intervention, and the like—have no validity in themselves, and indeed are none of them (many claims to the contrary notwithstanding) vital to any true religion. For such of us, supernaturalism and revealed religion are dead, because meaningless. Religion, in the light of psychological and anthropological science, is seen not as a divine revelation, but as a function of human nature. It is a very peculiar and very complicated function of human nature, sometimes noble, sometimes hateful, sometimes intensely valuable, sometimes a bar to individual or social progress. But it is no more and no less a function of human nature than fighting or falling in love, than law or literature.

WHAT DARE I THINK?

Let, then, the dead bury their dead. The task for us is to rejuvenate ourselves and our subject by a plunge into the waters of human nature, to study religion not as a problem of theology or scholastic logic, not as something divine or supernatural in contrast to the mundane and natural, but as an organic function, capable, like other human functions, of modification, training, and improvement.

Science too is, of course, a function of human nature. It arises out of the desire to know for knowing's sake; and it proves to be the only sure method for increasing our practical control over the world. Scientific laws are no longer looked upon as something existing apart from us which we chance to discover as we discover a Rosetta Stone or a new Codex, but as the most convenient way of classifying things and the way they happen. Nor is scientific knowledge absolute knowledge. So-called primary qualities, like mass and form, turn out to be just as much products of our construction, of the way we experience phenomena, as are so-called secondary qualities like smells or colours.

SCIENCE, RELIGION AND HUMAN NATURE

The world seems to boil down to vast numbers of tiny fields of force interacting with each other across space; but we are aware of it as consisting of things to be touched, seen, smelt, and heard. This is not to say that science is therefore fallacious; it gives us the most accurate picture of phenomena which we can obtain, and the accuracy of the picture is continually increasing. But, though the picture doubtless corresponds in some perfectly orderly way with reality, it is not a picture of reality, but of one aspect of our experience of reality. Science, in fact, is a way of ordering our experience; and it is, with its constant testing and reference back to the facts of experience, the only way by which we can progressively increase our knowledge and our control of the objective world.

As such, it has not only the right but the duty to provide the cosmic side of that intellectual scaffolding of religion which we call theology. It provides the background against which man's religious feelings and beliefs are to play their parts. And those feelings and beliefs themselves will be influenced by their background. Man believing himself the inhabitant of the Universe's central globe, created a few thousand years ago, brought salvation by the Son of his Creator, looking forward to a not-too-distant end of this terrestrial home, cannot well have the same religion as man knowing himself descended by slow evolution from the brutes, inhabitant of an insignificant appendage of one out of many million stars, with hundreds of thousands of years behind him, and tens or hundreds of millions before him.

But our chief concern is with the humanistic approach to religion—the consideration of religion as a function of the human organism, a natural product of human nature; and it is to this that we must return. There are many people who, though they claim to freethinking and independent judgment in religious matters, will not accept such an idea as possible, and many others who will say that they cannot see how religion can be defined in terms of human function. To them religion inevitably connotes the worship of an independent and divine Being; and the main emphasis in their thought is the relation of religion to the God instead of its relation to the man who practises it. They too are victims of the attitude of which I have already spoken—caught in the theological ideas of past ages, they have not yet succeeded in piercing beyond the products of religion to the religious impulse itself. They have accepted the orthodox idea of God at its face value, and have not perceived that God, in the current sense in which they use the word, is the creation of man.

But, you will ask, eliminate the idea of a Divine Person or Being to be worshipped, prayed to, or propitiated, and what remains of religion? A great deal, I would answer. For what all sorts and kinds of religion have in common is, first, a reaction of the human spirit to the facts of human destiny and the forces by which it is influenced; and, secondly, a reaction into which there enters a feeling of sacredness. This may seem so vague as to be no definition at all; yet religion is protean, and, like life, eludes precise or detailed definition. Life can scarcely be defined more specifically than as a capacity of a certain kind of matter for continued cyclical self-reproduction. But granted this general property, particular circumstances mould it into characteristic forms of the utmost concreteness, each vitally itself, and yet specifically interlocked with a specific environment and way of life, each with its own limitations, yet each alive and real. This general property of a certain kind of matter has permitted the development of oak-tree, toadstool, squirrel, and hawk, each gaining the matter for its self-reproduction in a different kind of way; has moulded the salmon to the water, the deer to the plains-ground, the swallow to the air; has produced creatures as differently organized as lobster, fish, and octopus, all equally well adapted to their surroundings, and yet each possessing its own type of organization, wholly different from that of the others; and, finally, has given origin to a true progress, in which we can discern higher and lower organizations, and trace the real advance

SCIENCE, RELIGION AND HUMAN NATURE

stand for a whole system of emotions and ideas, either because symbol and system have some property in common, as with the symbol of the lamb for Jesus, or the encircling wedding ring as symbol of the bond of marriage, or because the object has played a vital part in sacred events, as with the cross which has become charged with the whole burden of sacrifice and divine redemption.

Another different category of objects frequently invested with religious quality in early religions is that of animals. The motive here seems often to be mixed. Partly they are thought of as symbols of certain vital qualities, partly as formidable enemies or as necessities of existence, while, in addition, the primitive mind, as evidenced by the widespread totemic system, has for some obscure reason chosen to reverence an animal as ancestor of the enduring human clan.

This last motive for investing an object with sanctity is seen in pure form in ancestor-worship and kindred systems. But in such cases it is the vague indwelling spirit of the clan or family which is reverenced rather

WHAT DARE I THINK?

than its concrete, individual members. The chief reason for ascribing religious significance to actual human beings seems, in the first instance, to have been outstanding achievement. Later, owing to the complex interweaving of motives, set forth once and for all by Frazer in the *Golden Bough*, the headship of tribe or state comes to be fraught with intense magico-religious significance, often to such an extent as to make the life of its occupant a burden, or even to demand his ritual death. In these cases a true deification of the man has to greater or lesser extent taken place, and, even in such a high civilization as that of Imperial Rome, emperors were accorded divine honours.

Another type of religious significance adheres to men who occupy sacred offices, such as the Pope, or, indeed, the humblest ministers of many religions; and still another to those who achieve sanctity, or rather what is felt by the contemporary mind as sanctity, in their own persons—mystics, anchorites, fakirs, ascetics, saints.

We then come to a quite different group of

SCIENCE, RELIGION AND HUMAN NATURE

phenomena which have very commonly become invested with religious feeling—the biological crises of human existence, and notably those universal ones of birth and death, puberty and marriage. There are some peoples to whom even death seems invested with little religious feeling; important personages are buried with pomp, but ordinary folk are not supposed to be immortal, and their corpses may be thrown out without ceremony. But, in general, religious feeling has strongly impregnated these human occasions. The precise nature of the religious sentiment involved may differ much at different stages of development. Anthropologists seem agreed, for instance, that much of the marriage ceremonial among most primitive peoples is aimed at removing the possible evil influences of taking a stranger into the family, and, in fact, is concerned more with fear than with joy; but it contains a religious motive, just as much as does a Christian wedding ceremony (and just as little as does a wedding in a registry office).

Thoughts of the mystery of human destiny,

the incalculability of fate, the brevity of life, are natural and all but inevitable at such times, so that, even when the magical motive is abolished, these occasions continue to be natural objects for religious feeling. It is a familiar enough fact that, in many parts of Europe, the bulk of the peasantry, while bothering their heads very little about religion in general, yet insist passionately upon its presence on the scene at the crises of birth, marriage, and death. In a similar way, national triumphs or calamities are usually felt as demanding a religious celebration. Besides these special occasions there are recurrent moods and attitudes in human life which seem inevitably to become interwoven with religion. The most important of these is the individual's sense of dependence on powers other and greater than himself. Some writers, indeed, would make this the prime element in all religion, but this would wrongly exclude certain kinds of ecstasy and mystical experience from the religious category.

From this sense of dependence spring two

SCIENCE, RELIGION AND HUMAN NATURE

desires—for control over these powers, and for participation in them. The first finds expression in magic and sacrifice and conventional worship, the second in rites of communion or even identification with the god.

Our illustration of a religious celebration of victory or defeat leads us to another class of objects for religious feeling—the aspirations of the community. The most familiar example of this is provided in early Hebrew history: Jehovah began his career as the god of a fighting tribe, and only later developed into the God of Righteousness. He began as one among many similar and rival deities, and only gradually assumed the character of One and Universal God. Under the stress of war even modern Europe tended to revert to such ideas. There was a movement in Germany to hark back to the Teutonic pantheon, and references were made even in high places to 'our old German God.' And I myself have heard a cultivated English lady say that if Jesus had been alive in 1914 he would assuredly have enlisted on the side of the Allies.

WHAT DARE I THINK?

In modern nationalist States the frame of mind which engenders national gods tends to spill over into plain patriotism, which may be held with truly religious fervour, but has no organic connection with the professed religious system of the country or the professed religious beliefs of its citizens. Among primitive societies it tends to be merged into more general religious observances concerned with ancestor-worship and with fertility and other material benefits.

Then there are the very different bases of the religious life provided by concrete moral acts and spiritual experiences. There is an overpowering tendency in many minds to find in the giving up of what we desire and in self-mortification something which is inevitably tinged with sanctity. And the irrational tendency may be rationalized to make men feel that working for the good of others is not merely moral, but holy.

It is equally easy for prohibitions of what we desire to become invested with sanctity; hence arise elaborate tabu systems, and codes which are religious at the same time that

SCIENCE, RELIGION AND HUMAN NATURE

they are moral. Such irrational compulsions, fears, and inhibitions can easily be generated by the psychological mechanism of repression; they are common in children, and may, if exaggerated, distort the whole personality. In our civilized societies sex is the commonest fact of life round which this sacred ambivalence hangs in fullest force; but many and various are the raw materials here provided for the sense of sacredness to ferment in.

Finally, we come to less concrete but by no means less important fields over which religious emotion inevitably plays—the fields of abstract morality and truth. As is natural and unavoidable, the concrete is intertwined with the abstract, and, on the whole, precedes it in development. Many untutored savages would no more break an apparently irrational tribal tabu than would any of my readers commit a cold-blooded murder or deliberately pick a pocket; in both cases the prohibition is invested with an essentially religious compulsion, and to transgress would mean overcoming a non-rational and, indeed, sacred horror. But though the tabu might have no moral meaning in itself, though the man might never have attempted to think out why the tabu existed, or the rational significance of tabus in general, yet his concrete refusal to break a particular tabu still has an abstract basis ; even if no one were to see him and there were no risk of detection it would be *wrong*, he would say, to break it.

For man, in virtue of his fundamental and unique biological property of possessing general ideas, is thereby at a bound provided with abstract standards. To be able to say ' it is wrong ' assumes a distinction between right and wrong, and implies a standard of righteousness which exists in thought even if we never attain to it, and to us appears absolute. In the same automatic way are generated standards of truth or beauty or other general qualities. Such standards are only in appearance absolute, since they vary with the outlook and content of the mind which thinks them ; but they are abstract and general.

For our purpose, what is important is the

SCIENCE, RELIGION AND HUMAN NATURE

fact that these abstract and super-personal standards, whether consciously thought about or no, exist for human beings; and the further fact that they may readily become invested with religious feeling and be incorporated in the idea of God.

Very hastily and incompletely I have tried to set forth some of the chief objects and experiences which tend to become charged with religious feeling. From the point of view of theology, some of these are of more importance than others, since they have themselves become deified, or have been incorporated into the idea of God.

Every one knows Voltaire's dictum, that man made God in his own image. But the matter is not so simple as the great rationalist believed. Gods are more various than men; and many other ingredients beyond those taken from human nature enter into their composition. Even when at first sight direct deification seems to have occurred, as with the ascription of divinity to the sun or to a river, to an ancestral hero or an existing ruler, it will be found that in the manufacture of a divinity the concrete object or person and its qualities have almost always been blended with a further ingredient—the idea of influences, some straightforward and obvious, others mysterious and incalculable, affecting human destiny and welfare.

When religious ideas are more developed, other ingredients are often incorporated into the idea of divinity, and the mode of their organization becomes more elaborate. In addition to physical objects, any of the various forces and agencies of the non-human environment which affect human destiny may be organized in the god, including animals at the one extreme and general ' forces ' like fertility at the other ; and, in addition to individual human beings, we may find there the abstract ideas of morality, virtue, beauty, and truth, and also the aspirations of the community. And up to a very late stage good-sacred and bad-sacred have been mingled in the natures of men's deities.

We may not be able to agree precisely with Voltaire's views. But they embodied a pro-

SCIENCE, RELIGION AND HUMAN NATURE

found truth. All liberal theologians would to-day agree that the *idea* of god presented by any particular religion is man-made, whatever may be the reality behind the idea. And many left-wing thinkers would go further, and would say that for them the *idea of god* is all the god there is; that though the raw materials, so to speak, of which a god is composed exist independently of us, yet the actual making of gods is a purely human process, precisely similar to the process by which, according to our modern views, man makes natural laws out of the raw material provided by physical happenings.

But the genesis of gods is only part of a larger subject, the evolution of religion. Time and cumulative tradition enter into this; and the objects and ideas invested with religious emotion, of which I have just given a hasty catalogue, appear in wholly different guises and relations in different stages of the evolutionary process. My readers must, therefore, bear with me while I try once more to compress the incompressible, and analyse, however briefly, some of the chief stages and directions evident in religious evolution.

In religion, so long as it is alive, four aspects are blended. 1) There is immediate emotional experience; 2) there is ritual expression; 3) there is a connection with morality; and there is an intellectual scaffolding of ideas and beliefs. These can never be wholly disentangled. Even in the most personal of mystical experiences there is a setting of mind and body which is itself a ritual act; there is a background of consciously or unconsciously held beliefs which influence the form of the experience; there is an experience of rightness which overflows on to abstract views of morality and practical conduct. Ritual, again, if it be fulfilling its true mission, will itself be a source of religious feeling; but a ritual which is moving and significant to a mind imbued with one set of intellectual ideas will appear meaningless against another background of belief, and degraded mumbo-jumbo against yet another. Though the several aspects are inevitably inter-connected, their importance bulks very

SCIENCE, RELIGION AND HUMAN NATURE

differently in different religious systems, and each is capable of relatively independent development.

In the process of religious evolution we meet with a curious phenomenon. Progress in morality and ethical ideas is often quite independent of the orthodox religion of the day, and may even be independent of any religious feeling at all. And intellectual progress, in clear thinking and increased knowledge, has even less connection with religion. Yet it has been the changes in man's ethical and intellectual outlook which have chiefly determined the direction of religious evolution. And on the whole, especially in later centuries, it has been those more remote changes in regard to intellectual outlook which have had the greater effect.

At the risk of over-simplification, we can mark three main stages in the intellectual background of religion according to the predominance of three very different systems of beliefs. The first is the belief in magic; the second the belief in personal gods who control the world's affairs; the third, the modern scientific belief in the uniformity of nature and the impersonal working of natural laws.

Magic, as has often been insisted, is not of necessity religious in its origin or its nature. It is rather a forerunner of science, but one based on wrong premisses and faulty methods. But so long as man's thought remained in a low stage of development magic and religion were intimately, and for the time being inseparably, united.

In most cases magic is based in some degree on man's almost incurable habit of what psychologists call *projection*—the endowing of an object with some of the feelings or ideas which it arouses in us. It is in this way, it seems, that unfamiliar, portentous, or strange objects, such as meteorites or queer-shaped stones, may acquire magico-religious significance, just as toads, cauls, midnight, human bones, and other emotionally-charged ingredients enter into the recipes alike of savage, classical, and mediæval witchcraft.

The other necessary condition for the existence of belief in magic is the confused intuitive animism characteristic of many young children and most primitive tribes, which peoples their world with forces of will and caprice, malice and benevolence, akin to those they know in their own persons and other human beings. This depends largely on reasoning by analogy, and in part on a somewhat different form of projection. It is the first step towards personification. But it is of some importance to remember that, even without any personification, the 'charging' of objects with emotion and supposed power, by means of straightforward projection, will and does take place in any intellectual conditions under which magic can flourish.

The next period is the period of gods. Belief in gods may, and usually does, exist in the previous stage. But they often play a subordinate rôle in the current religion (in several tribes, for instance, a beneficent creator is recognized, but is rarely worshipped or propitiated, just because he is beneficent, and it is so much more important to propitiate the powers that might do you evil); and in any case they merely constitute focal points or specializations, so to speak, in the general system of magical influence. Similarly, belief in magic may, and usually does, persist into the succeeding stage. But the prime intellectual emphasis has passed to the personal deity; magic becomes a tool of the gods or demons, or else a subsidiary, more or less independent, system, which, as in astrology, may lose most of its connection with religion, or, as in witchcraft, may become associated only with the 'bad-sacred.'

In this stage of thought there are, of course, many sub-grades, and many different directions of progress. There exist all gradations from the innumerable fiddling little deities of Roman religion to the rigid monotheism of Judaism or Islam; from the monstrous pantheon of Egypt or Hindu India to the shining human gods of Greece or Scandinavia.

Almost without exception, however, much of the task earlier demanded of magic is in this stage transferred to the worship of the gods. Destiny is no longer thought of as the product of more or less impersonal forces,

SCIENCE, RELIGION AND HUMAN NATURE

mysterious, but in the main amenable to proper treatment by magic; it is now for the most part under the control of these personal divinities (though, as we know from Greek mythology, a relic of the former view survived in modified form in the belief that even the gods were subject to Fate). What is now important is to gain the favour of Deity; and rituals of praise, prayer, and propitiation take the place of the more impersonal and materialistic methods of pure magic.

The more spiritually-minded will always react against the cruder manifestations of this spirit. One or other of two rather different results may follow. Either the idea of the god itself may suffer a change and a purification, as was the result of the protests of the Hebrew prophets against the crudity of material sacrifice and the narrowly nationalist view of Jehovah. Or the reaction may be more fundamental, and lead men to search for salvation and religious fulfilment in their own souls and their own way of life rather than in the service of a deity conceived of as a separate overruling being. Most of the great mystics and many of the inspired moralists of religious history have been subject to this reaction. But its two greatest exemplars were Jesus and the Buddha. Jesus said: 'The Kingdom of Heaven is within you.' And Buddha went even further. Not only did he make salvation—or, as we had better say to avoid misunderstanding, the achievement of true and religious satisfaction—dependent upon progress along the Path, which was a path of inner spiritual achievement, but in his teaching there is no reference at all to an external god.

It is noteworthy that, in either case, the purely spiritual and personal side of the teacher's message, though not lost, has been smothered with growths of the very kind against which he was protesting. Christianity became the greatest institutional religion which the world has seen, with an elaborate scheme of externalized salvation. And Buddhism in the land of its birth succumbed to the greater objectivity of Hindu polytheism, and elsewhere survives institutionally only in degraded and wholly altered

SCIENCE, RELIGION AND HUMAN NATURE

form. The facts are significant. The intellectual framework of human thought was not ready for the stresses which this psychological and personal conception of religious fruition inflicted upon it. While ignorance and fear still could make it seem possible or likely that the control of events in this world and the next lay in the hands of superhuman beings with their own feelings and arbitrary wills, humanity not unnaturally felt it unsafe and unwise to abandon the propitiation of these powers in favour of the more arduous cultivation of the spirit, which, it seemed, was to be its own reward.

The premiss of supernatural beings endowed with consciousness and personality (or attributes of the same order), and with control over the fate of the world and the destiny of souls, has been the fundamental premiss of all Western religious thought for several thousand years. Yet within the limitations imposed by this premiss much development, mostly progressive, has taken place. One major development has been primarily logical and intellectual. It is the trend towards unity and universality. If you believe in many gods you leave a residuum of compromise and illogicality in the government of the world. If the postulate of divinity be accepted it will be very hard to avoid making your divinity all-powerful, and therefore unitary, eternal, and universal, though the unifying process may take centuries.

A second has been primarily moral and ethical; it is the trend towards eliminating the bad-sacred from the nature of God, and the consequent ascription to him of omniscience, moral perfection, and ultimate benevolence. Again, if you believe that life, either in this world or the next, is worth living, and if you ascribe any moral qualities to God, you have initiated a process which can scarcely fail to culminate in the conception of an ethically perfect god.

And a third has been, we may say, primarily philosophical. It is the tendency to dehumanize God by denying him many attributes of ordinary human personality, and ascribing qualities which we may call superpersonal: qualities akin to those of personality, but infinitely above it, and not to be properly grasped by limited creatures like human individuals.

It is clear that, in the course of these three intertwined processes, a great many of the more human and engaging properties of the early gods of naïve men will be philosophized away.

CHAPTER VII

Science and the Future of Religion

IN the last chapter, after setting forth something of the psychological bases of religion, I endeavoured to trace certain of the main phases and influences of its evolution.

The evolution of the higher organisms has often been adventurous and surprising. What transformations our own life-stream has experienced, from worm-like chordate to armoured vertebrate, from finny fish to crawling land-beast, from scaly reptile to hairy mammal, from tree-dwelling monkey to two-legged naked man! But the transformations of human religion have been scarcely less extraordinary. Could a Martian philosopher have the opportunity of examining the mental equipment of some cultured adult representatives of our modern civilization, we may doubt that he would be able to

SCIENCE AND THE FUTURE OF RELIGION

deduce humanity's religious past, any more than he would be likely to guess that in their physical past they had traversed an egg-laying phase or a fish-like phase. For assuredly it was a strange nexus of ideas and emotions which created the sacred Priest-King, never allowed to set foot to ground; or produced the corps of temple prostitutes; or combined limbs and features of beasts and men in monstrous deities; or demanded the constant immolation of human victims, as in Aztec Mexico.

So we may feel sure that the religious impulse, with its manifold roots reaching into every corner of the human organism, is not likely to evolve according to any definite plan. Just when it seems to be growing tamed by logic, it bursts forth in some new form, intellectually exotic or emotionally unrestrained. So in our own time, for instance, we have seen the reaction against the too logical spirit of rationalism and the comfortable course of orthodoxy, in the shape of the uncritical excesses of Spiritualism and the strange fantasies of Christian Science.

However, if we are never likely to be able to prophesy the precise course of religious evolution in detail, there is at least some appearance of a general trend in the process, leading religious belief upwards through a series of main stages. Of these main stages we have attempted to distinguish three, and we have given a brief account of the characteristics of the first two.

We are now at the beginning of the third, the scientific, stage. After a bare three centuries of the scientific spirit we cannot expect our scientific view of the world to have attained any semblance of completeness; to the science of ten thousand years hence it will doubtless seem as patchy and insufficient as does early polytheism in comparison with developed scholastic theology. But the scientific approach involves a fundamental change of outlook, and the influence of that change is already apparent in many fields.

Its most obvious theological effect is this, that it renders either futile or illogical all straightforward personification of divinity, all conceptions of God which regard him

SCIENCE AND THE FUTURE OF RELIGION

as a separate being controlling the universe which he has created, all views which stress God's transcendence instead of his immanence.

In face of the advance of scientific understanding the controlling functions of God the Ruler, as they were confidently assumed by a simpler theology, have gradually dwindled away. With final realization of the universality of natural law and its automatic, inevitable workings, such a god is reduced to the position of a spectator, benevolent perhaps, but ineffective, of the workings of the cosmic machine. His only possible function is that he may have created the machine; and, of course, if he is all-wise, he will then have known exactly how it was going to work. But for the rest his sole occupation throughout eternity is to enjoy the verification of his predictions.

This, it appears to me, is the only logical outcome of the belief in a personal or super-personal absolute god who is external to his world, when it is confronted with modern science. Instead of ruling a kingdom he merely holds a watching brief—of which he never utilizes the results. The only two avenues of escape from this conclusion are, first, that he sometimes does interfere; and, secondly, that he does not know the future, because of human freewill. And both are barred, for the first is contradicted by scientific knowledge; and, if the second be true, God is not absolute, and in any case is in no less futile a position.

Theology is well aware of this, and as a result has come to lay more and more stress on the immanent aspect of God, and on his super-personal aspects, which make of his nature something profoundly different from mere human personality. If you read theological works by liberal scholars within the Protestant Churches, for instance, you will find accounts of God which are as modernist as could be desired, and have left behind every shred of the anthropomorphism of earlier and cruder days. Gone is the bearded Jehovah, gone is Milton's conversational God the Father, and in their place are creative principles, immanent spirit, divine purpose

SCIENCE AND THE FUTURE OF RELIGION

informing the slow movement of evolutionary progress, and so forth.

I have been accused of ignorance of these modern theological tendencies because I have continued to attack the anthropomorphic idea of God and all that is implicit in it. But the truth of the matter is that so long as the outworn ideas continue to stand uncorrected, implicit in all that is most sacred and essential in the Christian creeds and liturgy, so long must liberal Christian theologians endure being told that they are trying the impossible game of having their cake and eating it. The creeds, the words of every book of the Bible, the very fact of petitionary prayer, the language of any and every hymnal—all implicitly, or more usually explicitly, assert a belief in a personal God, a God who can survey from the outside the world he has made, who controls its normal workings and can miraculously interfere with them, who listens to prayer and may grant its petitions, who can be pleased or wrathful, who can purpose and plan, who deliberately sent his son into this world to save sinners.

WHAT DARE I THINK?

Liberal theologians tell us, quite correctly, that this is all an outcome of the primitive habit of thought of earlier generations and of the limitations of language. This is myth, that is symbol; this a valiant attempt to express the inexpressible, that an unfortunate inexactitude.

But so long as the plain statements in Bible and Prayer Book stand uncorrected and unannotated in their central position, so long will the Churches be in the awkward position of standing with one leg on either side of a nasty gulf; or, if you prefer a time-honoured metaphor, of attempting to ride two horses at once. Its leaders will believe one thing, the mass of adherents something not merely different in being simpler, but radically different in nature.

I may perhaps illustrate what I mean by two recent extracts from the newspapers. In the *Times* of September 13, 1930, was a long letter from the veteran Canon J. M. Wilson (one of the few living men who read the *Origin of Species* on its publication—and, what is more, felt it not as a blow to religion, but a

SCIENCE AND THE FUTURE OF RELIGION

vital contribution to thought) [1] on the Report of the Lambeth Conference on the Doctrine of God. He writes of the Report that it places the Creeds ' quietly in their proper historical setting. . . . Not neglecting or treating as of no importance, but rather treating the Creeds as they are, as educational stages of our Faith, as preparatory, as symbolical, as temporary, and approximate. . . . It recognizes that there is no finality yet in sight ; . . . it greatly enlarges the limits of the Church.' And yet, within the last few years, we have had the South African heresy trial and the Dayton Evolution case !

The other was a Press message which informed us that the Archbishop of Naples had publicly stated that the recent Italian earthquake, in which many unfortunate people lost their lives, was God's way of showing that he disapproved of the immorality of women's dress. How the Archbishop knew that the divine protest was directed against feminine fashions and not against the Fascist

[1] Alas, since these lines were written, Canon Wilson has died.

dictatorship, for instance, or the suppression of free speech in Italy, is not clear ; but that does not concern us. What concerns us is that the Christian Church can include views of the universe as radically different as those of the Archbishop of Naples and Canon Wilson, as those of the Anglican bishops assembled at Lambeth and the heresy-hunting Fundamentalists of Tennessee ; and that these views of the universe, these theologies, *are* radically different, as different as those of classical polytheism and early Christianity, as different as those of a believer in magic and a disciple of scientific method.

To my mind, the dilemma has come from a partial but incomplete realization, on the part of the more liberal theologians, of the implications of the scientific revolution. They have realized its implications in the domain of lifeless matter and in the field of evolution, but not in psychology and its consequences for comparative religion.

Personally, I believe that what is at fault is the fundamental postulate of the ordinary theistic view—the postulate that its god, however different in nature from ourselves, is a unitary being whose existence and unity are independent of human minds and thoughts. I believe, in fact, that men have in very truth made the gods. On such a view, the raw materials of gods do exist independently in nature; but the finished product is man-made. For example, as I have tried to set forth in detail elsewhere, the three Persons of the Trinity and their co-existence in Unity can reasonably be interpreted as personifications and deifications of three aspects of experience. The First Person would then primarily embody man's reaction to the stern and sometimes apparently hostile forces of nature, those to which the world owes its creation, those which bring man into existence and remove him from it, incomprehensibly, without his desiring the one or the other. The Second Person would be in the main the embodiment of the personal, individual elements in religion; and the Third Person of the abstract qualities and standards perceived by the human mind—the spirit of truth, the spirit of goodness, the spirit of justice and mercy, and so on. And the union of the three Persons in one God is in part the outcome of man's logical mind and his craving for unity, partly the intuitive grasp of the principle (which modern science has done so much to confirm) that everything is indeed inter-connected, all things and all events in truth manifestations of a single underlying unity.

Obviously, such a statement of the case is at best incomplete. Many other elements have entered into the Trinitarian doctrine, and the characters of the three persons are not so sharply delineated as my crude suggestion would make them. This latter fact is not unnatural in view of the ascription of personality, or something akin to it, to all three. But I believe that some process of the sort has been at work to produce the differentiation between the three persons, and that when looked at in this light, the doctrine of the Trinity, which has seemed so irrational to generations of advanced thinkers, is irrational only because of the consequences of ascribing personality and independent existence to God. In the fundamental intuition behind it, Trinitarianism is truer than many apparently more logical systems. It cuts the Gordian knot of logic which demands that God shall be either transcendent or immanent by making one aspect of him—the First Person—primarily transcendent, another—the Third Person—primarily immanent. Thus it avoids the consequences of too much insistence on divine immanence, which, if given their head, run straight off into pantheism; and, on the other, those of over-emphasis upon transcendence, which tend to make of God either an arbitrary and alien ruler or a mere watcher above and beyond actual things and events. Then, by insisting on the simultaneous humanity and divinity of Christ, it lays full emphasis on the true sanctity potential in human nature—the essential divinity to be found in man. Finally, by presenting us with the three differentiated Persons, it does its best to avoid the artificial compression of the richness of religious experience into too unitary and rigidly logical a form. Under such compression, either some aspects of God drop out in favour of others and God becomes one-sided, or all attributes suffer a certain vagueness as the deity retreats in self-defence a little further from the irrational confusion, but rich and fertile multiplicity, of actual experience.

However, I am not concerned to defend Trinitarianism as such. Rather let us take it, and one or two others of the most elaborate and successful products of the theistic stage of religious development, and endeavour to see, if we can, what limitations there are in the way of their continued evolution, their adjustment to the changed intellectual climate of modern times. As other representatives let us choose the straightforward monotheism of Islam and the polytheism of classical Greece. Of the limitations of rigid monotheism I have already said something. It represents the triumph of logic and the desire for unity over the claims of actuality and real multiplicity. And when logic and unity get to work upon the concept of an independent deity, they either narrow him or thrust him out into vagueness or remoteness.

SCIENCE AND THE FUTURE OF RELIGION

Greek polytheism, on the other hand, is the most clear-cut embodiment of divine variety. Here are none of the theological transformation scenes characteristic of Hinduism, the dissolving views whereby one god is suddenly turned into an aspect of another. The only connections between the various deities are those of kinship and the fact that all are subject to the decrees of Até—Destiny. This Destiny is so impersonal and mysterious as to remain formless; but all the other inhabitants of the pantheon are clear-cut separate beings, with human form and personality. Each represents an aspect of human life, human ideals, or of the environing forces with which they come into contact. It was a more flexible system, and it provided for greater variety, than any monotheistic creed: to take one obvious example, the spirit of earthly love, deified by the Greeks, finds scant representation in the nature of the Mohammedan or the Christian deity. But it failed. It failed, so it seems, for two reasons. One was its logical defectiveness: the principle of unity was too weak. The other, perhaps more important, was the insufficiency of a personality of human type, even if idealized, to bear the weight of godhead. For incorporated in the idea of godhead are two sets of ideas which refuse to be contained by single personalities: the idea of the non-human forces of nature, and that of abstract and eternal standards and principles such as truth, morality, beauty.

In so far as there is a differentiation of Persons within the Trinity, Christian theology can symbolize a richer variety than any straightforward monotheism; in so far as it includes them in a single God, it can satisfy man's instinct for unity and represent the real unity of nature better than can any straightforward polytheism; and in so far as the essence which it ascribes to God, though of the same order as human personality, is yet far more embracing, and not fully to be comprehended by limited human minds, it can not only include more elements than any straightforward anthropomorphism, but also touch profounder mysteries, more imper-

SCIENCE AND THE FUTURE OF RELIGION

sonal depths. But the inherent limitations remain. For, when all is said, it is only the blending which has been more skilful; the ingredients, or at least the kind of ingredients, remain the same. Like Islam, only to a lesser extent, it is not varied enough; like Greek polytheism, only to a lesser extent, it introduces human personality or something akin to it throughout its construction, and this material proves, in the long run, not to be capable of supporting the other necessary ingredients of deity; and, like Islam and Greek polytheism and all other theologies in the deifying stage of religion, by ascribing to God an independent existence it exposes him to an ignominious fate at the hands of advancing science—either of being driven outwards into the impotence of remoteness, or dispersed into the equal impotence of indwelling ubiquitousness.

This latter alternative is adopted by those religious philosophers who conclude that the universe *is* God. But to them, and to those others who identify God with the philosophical Absolute, the Unknowable behind phenomena, the unifying principle in reality, and so forth, we may legitimately reply that their conclusions may be of great interest for philosophy, but have ceased to have any but the remotest bearing on religion. Such a God could not be worshipped or prayed to, could not arouse the intense emotion or ecstasy of mystical experience, and, in fact, has really no kinship with the actual gods of actual religions.

Where, then, does the solution lie? It would seem to lie in dismantling the theistic edifice, which will no longer bear the weight of the universe as enlarged by recent science, and attempting to find new outlets for the religious spirit. God, in any but a purely philosophical, and one is almost tempted to say a Pickwickian, sense, turns out to be a product of the human mind. As an independent or unitary being, active in the affairs of the universe, he does not exist.

The religious emotions of mankind, these many centuries, have flowed into the channels of deity. The forms which they have taken have been in large measure deter-

SCIENCE AND THE FUTURE OF RELIGION

mined by this idea of God or gods. To imagine, as many people do, that religion will cease to exist if the idea of an independent God ceases to exist is to be lamentably illogical. The religious emotions are a natural product of man's nature. Robbed of the outlet of deity, they will find other outlets; no longer moulded by the idea of God, they will be moulded by other concepts, and will manifest a fresh evolution into new forms. And chief among the concepts which will mould this new evolution will be the concepts of science. For knowledge is inevitably the most important raw material of theology.

Can we venture on any prophecy as to the lines which the reconstruction will take? I think we can, although with the proviso that all we can hope to see is the beginning of a development whose end may and doubtless will be as different from its beginning as is modernist Christian theology from ancient Egyptian polytheism. Science is yet young. In the coming centuries there are bound to be radical alterations in our ideas about space, time, energy, and matter; and still more radical alterations in our ideas about mind and its place in the scientific scheme.

<u>The first, and in a way most important</u>, ingredient of any religion congruous with science must be a reverent agnosticism concerning ultimates, and, indeed, concerning many things that are not ultimates. Man is a limited and partial creature, a product of material evolution. He is a relative being, moulded by the struggle to survive in particular conditions on a particular planet. We have no grounds for supposing that his construction is adapted to understand the ultimate nature or cause or purpose of the universe, and indeed every reason for supposing the contrary. Quite apart from that, we can be sure that there are whole realms of knowledge which he has not yet discovered. The truly religious man must be content not to know many things, of which those that most vitally concern our present quest are the ultimate nature and purpose of the universe, and the truth as to the survival of personality after death.

SCIENCE AND THE FUTURE OF RELIGION

The obverse of this state of mind is the refusal to mistake wish for fact, the strength of one's desire for a thing for proof that the thing exists. Most men desire immortality, and this is often adduced as evidence that man is immortal. But it is of the very essence of the scientific spirit to refuse admittance to desire and emotion in the quest for knowledge—save only the one desire of discovering more truth.

The most important characteristic of scientific method is its constant reference back to experience in the search for knowledge. This also rules out a conception which played an important part in mediæval theology—the idea that pure deductive reason and abstract principles, such as that of perfection, could tell one anything about the nature of things. For Aristotle and the Schoolmen, the heavenly bodies had to be arranged on spheres and to move in circles because these are perfect forms, while ellipsoids and parabolas are not. And from purely abstract principles, such as the goodness of God and the consequent perfection of the universe, all sorts of elaborate deductions were made.

There is, however, no reason why the universe should be perfect; there is, indeed, no reason why it should be rational. What exists exists; and acceptance is man's first task. 'I am that I am' is a far truer piece of theology than all the deductive philosophy of the scholastics.

A further consequence of the adoption of the scientific outlook must be the break with any rigid or fixed authority in religion, and a willingness to accept change. It has been a matter of frequent comment in recent years that, whereas change in scientific ideas is generally regarded as a mark of scientific progress, change in religious ideas is generally thought of as a mark of religious degeneration. The new conceptions of evolution and relativity are victories for science; but when the belief in miracles is abandoned in favour of natural law, or the theory of verbal inspiration and absolute rightness of the Bible dropped for one of progressive religious development, the majority of men,

SCIENCE AND THE FUTURE OF RELIGION

whether religious or no, still seem to look upon it as a defeat for religion. This comes solely from the part which dogmatism and false theories of revelation and authority have played in the past history of religion. <u>It is perfectly possible to be religious and yet to welcome change without forfeiting stability.</u> Science is always changing; <u>but it is not unstable, only progressive. If progress itself be looked upon as a sacred duty, progress becomes an element in religion, and religious change will no longer alarm and shock religious minds.</u>

Finally, it is obvious that with the abandonment of the idea of God as a single independent power, with a nature akin to personality, many current religious practices will become meaningless. There will be no room for services of intercession, for prayer in the ordinary sense, for fear of incomprehensible punishment, for propitiatory sacrifice, or for the worship that is regarded as agreeable to its recipient. Providence turns out to be wrongly named, and the Will of God resolves itself into a combination of the driving forces of nature with the spiritual pressure of abstract ideas and certain of the conscious and subconscious desires of man.

What, then, remains for future religion? In the first place, a recognition of the fact that the religious spirit is a permanent element in human nature and a potent driving-force; that if it is harnessed in ways which are intellectually wrong its results will eventually prove to be practically wrong; and that at present, for want of intellectually satisfactory outlets, the religious driving-force of a great many intelligent people is going to waste.

Next, a frank recognition that many of the functions of earlier types of religion are now as well or better carried out by other agencies. There was a time when the Church provided the art, music, and poetry of the community, whose needs in this respect are now in large measure satisfied by books, pictures, concerts, wireless, and the rest; a time when it provided the glamour, the rich illusion, and the escape from routine now gained in the theatre or the cinema; and the intel-

SCIENCE AND THE FUTURE OF RELIGION

lectual leadership, now given by philosophers, novelists, men of science, and other secular writers. This is recognized by churchmen like Dean Inge, who in his latest book writes: 'The more it leavens society the less, perhaps, will the power of the Church become, and the less need will be felt for a large Christian ministry.'

Yet the need for some specifically religious system to organize the driving-force of the specific religious emotion still remains. Even if we no longer symbolize the forces that mould man's destiny in the form of an independent God, we must acknowledge that to reflect on them, to attempt to think of them in their totality, and this in a spirit of reverence, is still a need and still a duty; and to do so is a truly religious activity, more than ever necessary in a democratic society. We must further acknowledge that to enable the rank and file of workaday humanity to achieve this some organization is necessary. There must be men and women who will give the major portion of their time to thinking of such things, to their explanation and exposition, to the guidance of enquiring or perplexed minds along the right path.

We must accept the obvious fact that for a great majority of people some form of religious service, in the sense of some organized communal gathering with a recognized procedure, is the best way of ensuring that they shall periodically escape from the pressure of routine and worldly cares and have an opportunity of seeing things *sub specie aeternitatis*, or at least in the longest view that is possible.

Prayer in the sense of petitions for benefits may be meaningless; but prayer in the sense of meditation guided by religious feeling, of a release of our deepest aspirations, an attempt to disentangle our desires and relate them to each other and to the impersonal and super-personal forces of the world and the human community we live in—that is both psychologically reasonable and spiritually efficacious. And here again the performance of such meditation in common is to many people a help; Moncure Conway himself was one of the first to substitute the practice for conventional prayer in a religious service.

SCIENCE AND THE FUTURE OF RELIGION

We ~~may~~ [Should] recognize that the sanctity of a building, a rite, a form of words, or a symbol, is not inherent, nor miraculously conferred by a supernatural power, but a product of our own minds. Yet this does not prevent us from recognizing that it exists, or preclude us from using this faculty of men of projecting their emotions into objects, in order to concentrate religious feeling and give it a common focus for many individuals.

We can no longer promise salvation in the conventional sense. But it is a simple fact that men and women can come to achieve a sense of harmony and peace, a conviction of the value of existence, a feeling that their relation with the world at large is no longer confused or meaningless, but right and significant; and any religion worthy the name will help them towards this. In the same way, no one can deny the existence of the sense of sin (though they will observe that the sense of sin is often exaggerated in highly moral people, and atrophied in the immoral), nor will they deny that through spiritual experiences the sufferer can escape from the gloom and horror and isolation of this feeling. To exaggerate the sense of sin, as is done by certain religious bodies, is unpardonable ; but to attempt to get rid of it by merely deadening it is as bad. It is a symptom that something is wrong ; and, when exaggerated, a symptom of a radically diseased soul. But religion, instead of exploiting it, can help to reduce it to its proper place as a warning signal.

So with the sense of grace, with conversion, with mystical experience. We need not attach the same meanings to them as are attached by current theology ; but to deny their existence as psychological facts is unscientific, to deny their value as spiritual experience is irreligious. Like much else, they can be abused ; but the infusion of the scientific outlook into religion can guard against that.

Mystical experience is an excellent example for our purpose. At one extreme you will find it asserted that such experience gives direct knowledge of or communion with the Absolute or with an external Deity ; at the

SCIENCE AND THE FUTURE OF RELIGION

other that it is a purely pathological phenomenon. A scientifically-based religion would say that neither of these views is true, but that mystical experience is a way of combining thought and feeling, inner and outer, which gives satisfaction in its own right, just as does feeling well, or making a scientific discovery, or looking at a beautiful landscape. The same quality enters into the experience of enjoying great poetry or art, or of falling in love ; the mystical experience, properly so-called, differs from this in that the emotional setting is preponderantly a religious one. But all have value in themselves, all are felt as sanctifying and deepening common existence, all help in the task of carrying on with the routine of every day.

By proclaiming the significance of such psychological facts, their value, and their possible danger and abuses, an organized religion can do a great deal to enrich men's spiritual life.

It would need far more space than I have at my command to deal fully with other aspects of religious life and their place in any non-theistic religion. Almost without exception, however, the elements and practices of the existing world-religions could be utilized by a religion which, abandoning the interpretation in terms of God, had adopted the scientific outlook as basis for its theology. But they would, of course, have to be transposed, as it were, into a new key, translated into new terms in accordance with the new outlook. Vicarious sacrifice, atonement, self-denial, and asceticism, the sense of inspiration or possession, the ecstatic or even orgiastic liberation from the bondage of sin, of self, or of convention, temporary or permanent retreat from the world, participation in inspiring ritual—these and many other things have their place in life, but will not find their right place unless they are helped to it by an organized religious system.

On the moral and practical side the new outlook will effect similar transvaluations. To take but one or two examples, the method of science will be recognized as the only method for translating man's wishes, however imperfectly, into actuality; and with the realization of the facts of evolution and heredity, and of the immensity of time ahead of the human race, eugenics will at once be seen to embody a religious ideal and a moral duty. Religion can continue to direct men's minds to aims which are not merely immediate; but in place of other-worldliness it will stress what in current terms would be called the realization of the Kingdom of God on earth.

But before I end I must speak of one point in which, as it seems to me, a non-theistic religion would have definite advantages over a theistic one. Theistic religion inevitably culminates in some form of monotheism; and the combination in the one God of the ideas of perfection and of unity with the attribution of moral qualities and other attributes of personality has inevitably, it would seem, a cramping effect. There is an oppression lurking in unity, a paralysis of life in logical perfection. G. M. Stratton, in his interesting book, *The Psychology of the Religious Life*, has admirably expressed this weakness of monotheism. 'The monotheist,' he writes, 'is apt to overprize the mere unity in his Ideal, forgetful that unity, if it grow too great, is tyrannous. ... Indeed, more than once in history a divine unity and concord has been attained at a cost of human colour and the rich play of interest and feeling. ... The Ideal is not merely a unity; it is quite as much a wealth and a diversity'—and so on.

I would go further. I would say that the theistic conception is confronted with an eternal dilemma, which only rare minds who can soar above appearances are capable of resolving. On one side is this danger of tyrannous compression; and if you avoid this, you run the risk of seeing your conception of divine personality evaporate into meaninglessness. If there is a single divine being, he must be all-powerful, all-knowing, all-good, with an eternal nature and an unchanging purpose. And if so, his nature becomes so different from ours that it no longer helps us; God becomes merely inscrutable.

SCIENCE AND THE FUTURE OF RELIGION

This is another way of saying that the logical Absolute is without significance for human affairs. It is without significance just because it is absolute and perfect, while the life of man, on its spiritual even more than on its physical aspect, is always and inevitably a development.

The standards which seem absolute are in reality only abstract; with increase of knowledge and insight their application alters, which is another way of saying that they alter. As for perfection, aesthetic and intellectual experience give us a clue. To discover or apprehend a particular truth, which may even be partial and destined to later supersession, can give a satisfaction which is complete in itself; a thousand different pictures or poems may give this complete satisfaction, and yet the absolute perfection of logic is obviously lacking in them. So there is a perfection in a bird or a deer or a flower, but it is neither a logical nor an absolute perfection.

Absolute and complete perfection, like absolute and complete truth, is to man—

relative and incomplete creature that he is—a purely abstract conception. But for any stage of a human being's development there are satisfactions which are perfect for that stage, because complete and harmonious relatively to his ideas and powers. Some such perfections are enduring, others transitory; all can be made the basis of more embracing perfections at a more developed stage.

But this is, in a sense, a digression. To the eye of science the difficulty of the theistic position would seem to come from its attempting to combine in the nature of one unitary being (besides properties derived from impersonal natural forces) properties derived from human personality and properties derived from pure logic and abstract standards. And the quality of absoluteness and completeness implicit in the one contradicts the quality of development inherent in the other.

If we no longer attempt to combine all these diverse properties in a single independent Being, the difficulties largely fall to the

SCIENCE AND THE FUTURE OF RELIGION

ground. The concept of development then comes to the front as the most vital, and the abstract values are seen in their true light, as inevitable methods of our thinking, which provide non-personal standards for the development of personalities. They have the utmost importance for this task, as they are the basis of any morality which is not purely individual; they are the girders and tie-beams which provide support and continuity to the mental life of the species. The individual inevitably seeks for sanctions and supports outside himself, greater than himself; these are the most important of such sanctions and supports. But they can now be kept in their proper place, as truly abstract principles, and therefore demanding to be clothed in concrete reality before they become significant.

The developed human personality is, in a strictly scientific sense, the highest product of evolution, the highest organization of which we have knowledge. And it is, therefore, the concept of development of personality which must occupy the centre of our religious scheme. Walt Whitman has expressed this idea in noble words:

> 'All parts away for the progress of souls;
> All religion, all solid things, arts, governments—all that was or is apparent upon this globe or any globe—falls into niches and corners before the procession of souls along the grand roads of the universe.'

But the 'progress of souls,' the enrichment and growth of personalities—that is something we can study in the world around us and in the lives of great men and women as recorded in books. And we shall see that courageous experiment makes for the enlargement of life, though it often (as in Moncure Conway's own life) leads to the abandonment of old principles for new; that mistakes are inseparable from progress; that variety of experience enriches life, often in unexpected ways, and may tumble a man out of a narrow unity into a broader and deeper unity which transcends the boundaries he was capable of seeing before his eyes were opened by new experience.

It is a commonplace of Christian theology that failure, sin, and suffering can be transmuted into things of value to life; and this is one of its greatest contributions to religious thought. It is only when it denies efficacy to all other means of effecting the transmutation save those prescribed by its theological scheme that it reveals its limitations.

The development of this theme would take us far afield. All I wish to stress here is that the capacity of the human mind and soul for enlargement, enrichment, and development is virtually unlimited, but that in the nature of things the immature mind has not realized many of the possibilities inherent in it; and that experiences of the most diverse and apparently irreconcilable nature can be and often are reconciled and made part of a fuller life. Provided that goodwill and sincerity and what we may call by the old name of natural piety are there, variety of experience is an asset. It is, indeed, right and proper not to attempt too much consistency, as this will almost invariably be found to be based on logic, yes—but on incomplete premisses.

One of the obvious attractions of Greek polytheism, for instance, was the variety of human activities and aspirations which it could accommodate within its boundaries. Freed from the necessity of propitiating or imitating a unitary being, a modern religion could revert to that rich variety; while its release from belief in arbitrary divine control would allow it to concentrate upon the task of vivifying and enhancing life by giving a sacramental quality to all these its various attributes and activities, instead of falsifying its mission and dissipating its energies in propitiation or magic mumbo-jumbo.

Unity and consistency have their rightful place in religion as in human nature; but the unity is more embracing than we perceive, the consistency a convenience rather than a necessity. We need a trust in the unifying activity of the growing mind and of the outer universe, deliberately encouraging a religion of variety, in the faith that the variety will be reconciled in ways often beyond our comprehension at the time.

* * * * * *

But after all the disputation is done and its dust has died away, there remains the

SCIENCE AND THE FUTURE OF RELIGION

central question : Do people want a new religion, or, at any rate, the only kind of new religion which we in this place would willingly see—namely, one with a scientific basis and outlook ? Men and women are deserting the religions which have a God. Will they want to join one without a God ?

I believe that many would. But only on certain conditions. One we have already devoted much time to discussing—that its intellectual outlook should tally with modern scientific knowledge, and should be willing to change and march forward as new knowledge altered the scientific outlook.

The next is that it shall satisfy to the fullest possible extent the psychological needs of the individual man and woman. On many issues it must remain agnostic, and therefore must enjoin stoicism ; but, as Professor Gilbert Murray has beautifully set forth in one of his essays, there is no quarrel between stoicism and religious feeling, and the stoical attitude has an important part to play in any developed religion.

Though it cannot give what to us seem

false or dubious assurances on certain matters, it still has a wide field before it. It can help people to rid themselves of their sense of helplessness and isolation by showing them that they have a place in the enduring community of thought and purpose, joy and suffering, constituted by mankind. It can organize the religious life, providing retreats and celebrations, instruction and ritual, which are not at the command of the unorganized individual. To take a simple example from the present day, the number of people who avail themselves of the open doors of certain London churches for a brief interval of peace and meditation is very large.

It can help to kill fear, and to achieve freedom from the sense of sin. It can reveal to its adherents unexpected richnesses, possibilities of their own nature of which they were ignorant. It could achieve this by studying the psychology of mystic experience and the sense of communion, and embodying its results in appropriate liturgies and in courses of devotional practice.

One of the chief motives which to-day

SCIENCE AND THE FUTURE OF RELIGION

bring recruits into the ranks of the Churches as ministers, missionaries, and church workers is the spirit of altruism, the desire to do something for others, which demands an outlet. And, naturally, any new organization could canalize that spirit in as many ways as do the old institutions, perhaps in more.

But it will never be a real force in human affairs unless, in addition to providing spiritual refuge and solace and the opportunity of doing miscellaneous good works, it makes some bold appeal to the moral sense and the imagination of humanity.

As I see the matter, the facts provided by science, which become theology when ordered in relation to a religious outlook—an outlook, that is to say, concerned with man's relation to the rest of the universe—show us two broad tendencies which are in a sense antagonistic, though both run their course in the same world-stuff. One is the tendency, epitomized for us in the second law of thermo-dynamics, of lifeless systems to run down into stagnation, into conditions where none of their energy is in available form. The other is the tendency, as embodied in the facts of evolution, of living matter to progress to ever higher levels of achievement, into forms which have more internal harmony, more external control, more intensity of mental life. And man, with his scale of values, is the culmination of this second trend. The categorical, or perhaps I had better say the psychological, imperatives within us bid us realize these values to the fullest extent. That is an internal guidance. And when we look for external guidance we find the advice reinforced by the facts of life's evolution. Our conscious values are both the climax and the symbol of our evolutionary history. To bury one's talent in a napkin is also to be false to the whole past of life. To work so that man, individually and collectively, shall progress towards greater control over nature, more harmonious development, and richer and fuller intellectual and emotional life, is to show oneself the heir of an upward movement that has lasted for a thousand million years, and may endure for

SCIENCE AND THE FUTURE OF RELIGION

still longer periods into the future. We are living matter ; and, though the purpose and fate of the universe as a whole is and may be for ever hidden from us, the past history of living matter gives us a partial clue, a direction which we must obey if we do not wish to falsify the destiny of life, that whole of which we are the culminating part.

Thus, whether looked at from the human or from the scientific point of view, a new religion cannot be a religion of negation, of death, of asceticism, of resignation. It must be a religion of life. It must make its first and greatest aim the enrichment of life. From the point of view of the individual's inner life, its message will be that life can be sacramental. The apprehension of truth or beauty ; suffering or sacrifice ; simple joy and simple health ; love, physical and spiritual alike ; ecstasy and discipline ; self-surrender and self-control—the most widely-differing aspects of life can become tinged with transcendent emotion, whereby ' we feel that we are greater than we know,' and come to experience a new value in existence.

WHAT DARE I THINK?

It can also help to give to life a purpose that lies beyond self. From the point of view of the community, the race and its advance must be the centre of emphasis. Who can doubt that the motive of work for the continuing race and the increase of its capacities for achievement and enjoyment could be charged with religious emotion, and so made the main conduit for the long-range moral aspirations of man?

Indeed, there is no other way in which the community's moral stirrings can be made to square with the natural theology provided by science, and there is no other way in which the present regrettable tendency to erect Nationalism into a religion can be defeated. Last year's Conway Memorial lecturer, Mr Laurence Housman, put this matter forcibly when he said : ' The great practical danger to the forward movement of Rationalism and the peace and liberty of human society lies . . . in the still growing religion of Nationalism, the religion which makes each individual State an end in itself, and to that subordinates truth, morality, justice, and even ordinary common sense.' I would agree, only I would say that it was an obstacle not only to Rationalism, but to any religious progress whatsoever.

And in many other positive ways our religion can have an influence upon what philosophers would call the increased realization of ultimate values by man, what current religious phraseology would call the growth of the Kingdom of God upon earth, what the plain man would call an enrichment of life.

Let us not attempt to be too cloistered. We do not want our religion to be merely a week-end cottage for the soul, merely a retreat from the rest of our life. It should provide such a retreat, true; but it should also do something much more important—namely, provide both a perspective and a focus for life as a whole, and an objective for our activities. A religion, in fact, to be successful must have a practical programme, even if it be one of the most general kind. Early Christianity had the practical programme of preparing its members for the Second Coming and the Last Judgment;

later Christianity, in general, of preparing for the life to come ; missionary Christianity, like Islam, of saving souls for the glory of God ; Buddhism, of escaping from the tortures of desire into the peace which is above desire.

The practical programme of any new religion must develop gradually. But some of the broad outlines shape themselves in the mind's eye. The body of its adherents must pledge themselves to work against certain things which seem to them less ultimate and valuable, or hostile to their own values—like war and narrow nationalism and obscurantism, and the supremacy of purely economic motives, and other-worldliness as opposed to this-worldliness, and *laissez-faire* : to work for certain other things which seem to them more ultimate and valuable, like freedom, tolerance of sincere experiment, the advancement of knowledge, race improvement, the preservation and creation of beauty, the removal of fear, and so on. But some programme it must have beyond the provision of means of stimulating the religious

SCIENCE AND THE FUTURE OF RELIGION

emotions once a week (though this has its place and its value), and a string of moral platitudes.

It will need many decades before any new religion is able to organize itself; but the time ripens, and the world's dislocation of thought and the strange confusion of ephemeral and partial creeds presage a new birth now as they did before the birth of Christianity. It is not likely that any one of us will see that new birth; or, if we do, we shall very likely not recognize it for what it is. But we can to the best of our ability work towards it by clear thinking and a generous trust in the riches hidden in human nature.

That was the method of Moncure Conway. The best tribute to his memory is to imitate him. But in so doing let us not forget that, though the method and the outlook remain the same, their adaptation and application must inevitably change. Perhaps the greatest contribution of science to religion is the realization that truth lies in the future as much as in the past; and this applies equally to moral truth and aesthetic truth as to intellectual truth. A religion based on science and on human nature must be a religion of life, and therefore must not be afraid of the greatest and most precious property of life—the property of development and progressive change.

Printed in Great Britain
by T. and A. CONSTABLE LTD.
at the University Press
Edinburgh

CPSIA information can be obtained at www.ICGtesting.com
Printed in the USA
LVOW03s2055141114

413753LV00018B/580/P